Mountain Biking
the
Midwest

Dennis Coello's America by Mountain Bike Series

Mountain Biking
the
Midwest

*Dennis Coello's America by
Mountain Bike Series*

*Ohio
Indiana
Illinois*

Dave Shepherd

Foreword, Introduction, and Afterword
by Dennis Coello, Series Editor

Formerly *The Mountain Biker's Guide
to the Midwest*

Menasha
Ridge Press

FALCON™

© 1995 by Dave Shepherd
All rights reserved
Printed in the United States of America
Published by Menasha Ridge Press and Falcon Press
First Edition, first printing
Reprinted 1996

Library of Congress Cataloging-in-Publication Data

ISBN 1-56044-458-4

Maps by Tim Krasnansky
Cover photo by Dennis Coello

Menasha Ridge Press
3169 Cahaba Heights Road
Birmingham, Alabama 35243

Falcon Press
P.O. Box 1718
Helena, Montana 59624

 Text pages printed on recycled paper

CAUTION

Outdoor recreational activities are by their very nature potentially hazardous. All participants in such activities must assume the responsibility for their own actions and safety. The information contained in this guidebook cannot replace sound judgment and good decision-making skills, which help reduce risk exposure, nor does the scope of this book allow for disclosure of all the potential hazards and risks involved in such activities.

Learn as much as possible about the outdoor recreational activities you participate in, prepare for the unexpected, and be safe and cautious. The reward will be a safer and more enjoyable experience.

*For Terri, Ian, and Kyle, who were
always waiting patiently at the trailhead*

Table of Contents

NOTE: The 708 area code for phone numbers listed in rides 35, 36, and 40-42 will change to 630 on August 3, 1996.

Chicago Area: Forest Preserves and Parks

Rockford

Peoria

East Central Illinois

Shawnee National Forest

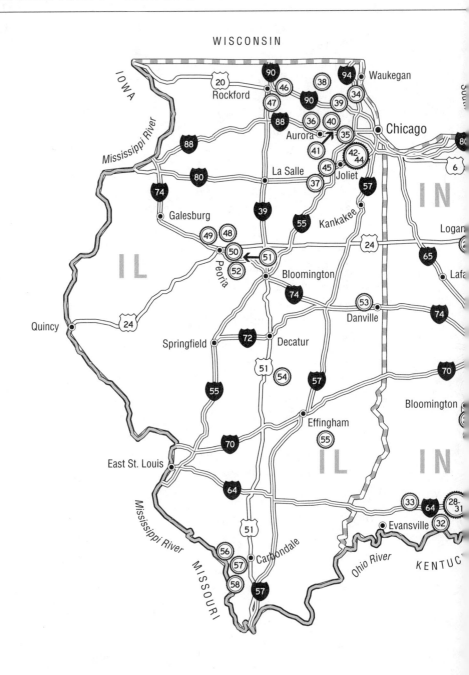

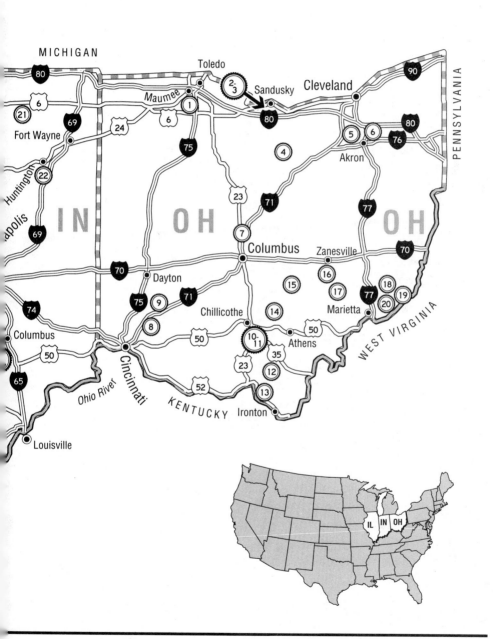

List of Maps

AMERICA BY MOUNTAIN BIKE *MAP LEGEND*

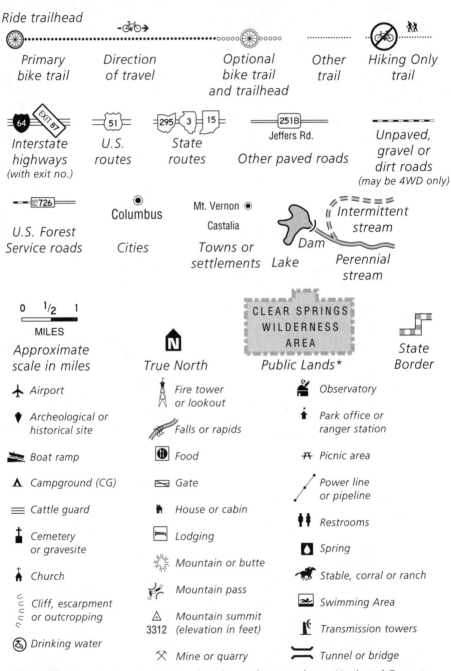

Ride trailhead

Primary bike trail

Direction of travel

Optional bike trail and trailhead

Other trail

Hiking Only trail

Interstate highways (with exit no.)

U.S. routes

State routes

Other paved roads — Jeffers Rd.

Unpaved, gravel or dirt roads (may be 4WD only)

U.S. Forest Service roads — 726

Cities — Columbus

Towns or settlements — Mt. Vernon, Castalia

Lake — Dam

Intermittent stream

Perennial stream

Approximate scale in miles — 0 ½ 1 MILES

True North — **N**

Public Lands* — CLEAR SPRINGS WILDERNESS AREA

State Border

✈ Airport

♥ Archeological or historical site

Boat ramp

▲ Campground (CG)

≡ Cattle guard

† Cemetery or gravesite

♠ Church

Cliff, escarpment or outcropping

Drinking water

Fire tower or lookout

Falls or rapids

Food

Gate

House or cabin

Lodging

Mountain or butte

Mountain pass

△ Mountain summit
3312 (elevation in feet)

⚒ Mine or quarry

Observatory

Park office or ranger station

Picnic area

Power line or pipeline

Restrooms

Spring

Stable, corral or ranch

Swimming Area

Transmission towers

Tunnel or bridge

*Remember, private property exists in and around our National Forests.

Foreword

Welcome to *America by Mountain Bike*, a 20-book series designed to provide all-terrain bikers with the information they need to find and ride the very best trails everywhere in the mainland United States. Whether you're new to the sport and don't know where to pedal, or an experienced mountain biker who wants to learn the classic trails in another region, this series is for you. Drop a few bucks for the book, spend an hour with the detailed maps and route descriptions, and you're prepared for the finest in off-road cycling.

My role as editor of this series was simple: First, find a mountain biker who knows the area and loves to ride. Second, ask that person to spend a year researching the most popular and very best rides around. And third, have that rider describe each trail in terms of difficulty, scenery, condition, elevation change, and all other categories of information that are important to trail riders. "Pretend you've just completed a ride and met up with fellow mountain bikers at the trailhead," I told each author. "Imagine their questions, be clear in your answers."

As I said, the *editorial* process—that of sending out riders and reading the submitted chapters—is a snap. But the work involved in finding, riding, and writing about each trail is enormous. In some instances our authors' tasks are made easier by the information contributed by local bike shops or cycling clubs, or even by the writers of local "where-to" guides. Credit for these contributions is provided, when appropriate, in each chapter, and our sincere thanks goes to all who have helped.

But the overwhelming majority of trails are discovered and pedaled by our authors themselves, then compared with dozens of other routes to determine if they qualify as "classic"—that area's best in scenery and cycling fun. If you've ever had the experience of pioneering a route from outdated topographic maps, or entering a bike shop to request information from local riders who would much prefer to keep their favorite trails secret, or know how it is to double- and triple-check data to be positive your trail info is correct, then you have an idea of how each of our authors has labored to bring about these books. You and I, and all the mountain bikers of America, are the richer for their efforts.

You'll get more out of this book if you take a moment to read the Introduction explaining how to read the trail listings. The "Topographic Maps" section will help you understand how useful topos will be on a ride, and will also tell you where to get them. And though this is a "where-to," not a "how-to" guide, those of you who have not traveled the backcountry might find "Hitting the Trail" of particular value.

In addition to the material above, newcomers to mountain biking might want to spend a minute with the glossary, page 194, so that terms like *hardpack, single-track,* and *water bars* won't throw you when you come across them in the text.

Finally, the tips in the Afterword on mountain biking etiquette and the land-use controversy might help us all enjoy the trails a little more.

All the best.

Dennis Coello
St. Louis

Preface

If your perception of Illinois, Indiana, and Ohio is of cornfields, I've got news for you: you're partly right. These Great Lakes states are known for agriculture, but the geographic diversity might surprise you. Having spent most of my life in northeastern Illinois, I am proud of my flatland heritage. But in reality, I was living in only half the dichotomy. Southern Illinois is a different animal. Keep in mind that Illinois borders Kentucky, and no one would ever accuse Kentucky of being flat. The same holds true of Indiana and Ohio. In northern Indiana, you'll find the white, sand dune beaches of Lake Michigan, but in the southern part of the state, the rolling hills take over. The busy, industrialized metropolises in northern Ohio are a sharp contrast to the bends and curves of the foothills along the West Virginia border.

Is this region like the Appalachian Mountains? No. Is it the Rockies? Certainly not. But don't let that deter you from mountain biking in Ohio, Indiana, and Illinois. You'll be pleasantly surprised by the riding you'll find here. You won't find climbs of several thousand feet, but the climbs you will encounter are just varied enough to keep it interesting. Even the predominately flat regions in the north yield pockets where the rides make up in technical challenges what they lack in elevation.

While compiling the rides in this book, I sought every permutation and combination I could find: long and difficult, short and difficult, long and easy, short and easy. In essence, there is something for everyone here. At times I felt like Siskel and Ebert composing their list of the top ten movies of the year: you can never please everyone. Each rider has his or her personal favorites, and choosing the rides that appear in this book was no easy task. I hope you'll find them as diverse and intriguing as I have.

One final point. It's interesting to note the contrast between the ruggedness of mountain biking as a sport and the sensitivity of land access. In the course of researching this guide, I found that certain trails closed down while others opened to mountain bikes. Mountain biking is a relatively new phenomenon in the region, and land managers are still determining their future mountain bike policies. I can only echo Dennis's comments about proper trail etiquette in the Afterword. If we're going to see mountain biking survive, it's up to us all to treat the land—and other trail users—with respect.

Happy trails!

Dave Shepherd

Mountain Biking
the
Midwest

Dennis Coello's America by Mountain Bike Series

Introduction

TRAIL DESCRIPTION OUTLINE

Information on each trail in this book begins with a general description that includes length, configuration, scenery, highlights, trail conditions, and difficulty. Additional description is contained in eleven individual categories. The following will help you understand all of the information provided.

Trail name: Trail names are as designated on United States Geological Survey (USGS) or Forest Service or other maps, and/or by local custom.

Length: The overall length of a trail is described in miles, unless stated otherwise.

Configuration: This is a description of the shape of each trail—whether the trail is a loop, out-and-back (that is, along the same route), figure eight, trapezoid, isosceles triangle, or if it connects with another trail described in the book.

Difficulty: This provides at a glance a description of the degree of physical exertion required to complete the ride, and the technical skill required to pedal it. Authors were asked to keep in mind the fact that all riders are not equal, and thus to gauge the trail in terms of how the middle-of-the-road rider—someone between the newcomer and Ned Overend—could handle the route. Comments about the trail's length, condition, and elevation change will also assist you in determining the difficulty of any trail relative to your own abilities.

Condition: Trails are described in terms of being paved, unpaved, sandy, hard-packed, washboarded, two- or four-wheel-drive, single-track or double-track. All terms that might be unfamiliar to the first-time mountain biker are defined in the Glossary.

Scenery: Here you will find a general description of the natural surroundings during the seasons most riders pedal the trail, and a suggestion of what is to be found at special times (like great fall foliage or cactus in bloom).

Highlights: Towns, major water crossings, historical sites, etc., are listed.

General location: This category describes where the trail is located in reference to a nearby town or other landmark.

Elevation change: Unless stated otherwise, the figure provided is the total gain and loss of elevation along the trail. In regions where the elevation variation is not extreme, the route is simply described as flat, rolling, or possessing short steep climbs or descents.

Season: This is the best time of year to pedal the route, taking into account trail

1

condition (for example, when it will not be muddy), riding comfort (when the weather is too hot, cold, or wet), and local hunting seasons.

Note: Because the exact opening and closing dates of deer, elk, moose, and antelope seasons often change from year to year, riders should check with the local Fish and Game department, or call a sporting goods store (or any place that sells hunting licenses) in a nearby town before heading out. Wear bright clothes in fall, and don't wear suede jackets while in the saddle. Hunter's-orange tape on the helmet is also a good idea.

Services: This category is of primary importance in guides for paved-road tourers, but is far less crucial to most mountian bike trail descriptions because there are usually no services whatsoever to be found. Authors have noted when water is available on desert or long mountain routes, and have listed the availability of food, lodging, campgrounds, and bike shops. If all these services are present, you will find only the words "All services available in . . ."

Hazards: Special hazards like steep cliffs, great amounts of deadfall, or barbed-wire fences very close to the trail are noted here.

Rescue index: Determining how far one is from help on any particular trail can be difficult due to the backcountry nature of most mountain bike rides. Authors therefore state the proximity of homes or Forest Service outposts, nearby roads where one might hitch a ride, or the likelihood of other bikers being encountered on the trail. Phone numbers of local sheriff departments or hospitals have not been provided because phones are almost never available. If you are able to reach a phone, the local operator will connect you with emergency services.

Land status: This category provides information regarding whether the trail crosses land operated by the Forest Service, Bureau of Land Management, a city, state, or national park, whether it crosses private land whose owner (at the time the author did the research) has allowed mountain bikers right of passage, and so on.

Note: Authors have been extremely careful to offer only those routes that are open to bikers and are legal to ride. However, because land ownership changes over time, and because the land-use controversy created by mountain bikes still has not completely subsided, it is the duty of each cyclist to look for and to heed signs warning against trail use. Don't expect this book to get you off the hook when you're facing some small-town judge for pedaling past a "Biking Prohibited" sign erected the day before. Look for these signs, read them, and heed the advice. And remember there's always another trail.

Maps: The maps in this book have been produced with great care, and, in conjunction with the trail-following suggestions, will help you stay on course. But as every experienced mountain biker knows, things can get tricky in the backcountry. It is therefore strongly suggested that you avail yourself of the detailed information found in the 7.5 minute series USGS (United States Geological Survey) topographic maps. In some cases, authors have found that specific Forest Service or other maps may be more useful than the USGS quads, and tell how to obtain them.

Finding the trail: Detailed information on how to reach the trailhead, and where to park your car is provided here.

Sources of additional information: Here you will find the address and/or phone number of a bike shop, governmental agency, or other source from which trail information can be obtained.

Notes on the trail: This is where you are guided carefully through any portions of the trail that are particularly difficult to follow. The author also may add information about the route that does not fit easily in the other categories. This category will not be present for those rides where the route is easy to follow.

ABBREVIATIONS

The following road-designation abbreviations are used in the *America by Mountain Bike* series:

CR	County Road
FR	Farm Route
FS	Forest Service road
I-	Interstate
IR	Indian Route
US	United States highway

State highways are designated with the appropriate two-letter state abbreviation, followed by the road number. *Example:* OH 93 = Ohio State Highway 93.

Postal Service two-letter state codes:

AL	Alabama		IA	Iowa
AK	Alaska		KS	Kansas
AZ	Arizona		KY	Kentucky
AR	Arkansas		LA	Louisiana
CA	California		ME	Maine
CO	Colorado		MD	Maryland
CT	Connecticut		MA	Massachusetts
DE	Delaware		MI	Michigan
DC	District of Columbia		MN	Minnesota
FL	Florida		MS	Mississippi
GA	Georgia		MO	Missouri
HI	Hawaii		MT	Montana
ID	Idaho		NE	Nebraska
IL	Illinois		NV	Nevada
IN	Indiana		NH	New Hampshire

NJ	New Jersey	SD	South Dakota
NM	New Mexico	TN	Tennessee
NY	New York	TX	Texas
NC	North Carolina	UT	Utah
ND	North Dakota	VT	Vermont
OH	Ohio	VA	Virginia
OK	Oklahoma	WA	Washington
OR	Oregon	WV	West Virginia
PA	Pennsylvania	WI	Wisconsin
RI	Rhode Island	WY	Wyoming
SC	South Carolina		

TOPOGRAPHIC MAPS

The maps in this book, when used in conjunction with the route directions present in each chapter, will in most instances be sufficient to get you to the trail and keep you on it. However, you will find superior detail and valuable information in the 7.5 minute series United States Geological Survey (USGS) topographic maps. Recognizing how indispensable these are to bikers and hikers alike, many bike shops and sporting goods stores now carry topos of the local area.

But if you're brand new to mountain biking you might be wondering, "What's a topographic map?" In short, these differ from standard "flat" maps in that they indicate not only linear distance, but elevation as well. One glance at a "topo" will show you the difference, for "contour lines" are spread across the map like dozens of intricate spider webs. Each contour line represents a particular elevation, and at the base of each topo a particular "contour interval" designation is given. Yes, it sounds confusing if you're new to the lingo, but it truly is a simple and wonderfully helpful system. Keep reading.

Let's assume that the 7.5 minute series topo before us says "Contour Interval 40 feet," that the short trail we'll be pedaling is two inches in length on the map, and that it crosses five contour lines from its beginning to end. What do we know? Well, because the linear scale of this series is 2,000 feet to the inch (roughly two and three-fourths inches representing 1 mile), we know our trail is approximately four-fifths of a mile long (2 inches x 2,000 feet). But we also know we'll be climbing or descending 200 vertical feet (5 contour lines x 40 feet each) over that distance. And the elevation designations written on occasional contour lines will tell us if we're heading up or down.

The authors of this series warn their readers of upcoming terrain, but only a detailed topo gives you the information you need to pinpoint your position exactly on a map, steer yourself toward optional trails and roads nearby, plus let you know at a glance if you'll be pedaling hard to take them. It's a lot of information for a very low cost. In fact, the only drawback with topos is their size—several feet square. I've tried rolling them into tubes, folding them carefully, even cutting them into blocks and photocopying the pieces. Any of these systems is a pain, but no matter how you pack the maps you'll be happy they're along. And you'll be even happier if you pack a compass as well.

In addition to local bike shops and sporting goods stores, you'll find topos at major universities and some public libraries, where you might try photocopying the ones you need to avoid the cost of buying them. But if you want your own and can't find them locally, write to:

USGS Map Sales
Box 25286
Denver, CO 80225

Ask for an index while you're at it, plus a price list and a copy of the booklet *Topographic Maps*. In minutes you'll be reading them like a pro.

A second excellent series of maps available to mountain bikers is that put out by the United States Forest Service. If your trail runs through an area designated as a national forest, look in the phone book (white pages) under the United States Government listings, find the Department of Agriculture heading, and then run your finger down that section until you find the Forest Service. Give them a call and they'll provide the address of the regional Forest Service office, from which you can obtain the appropriate map.

TRAIL ETIQUETTE

Pick up almost any mountain bike magazine these days and you'll find articles and letters to the editor about trail conflict. For example, you'll find hikers' tales of being blindsided by speeding mountain bikers, complaints from mountain bikers about being blamed for trail damage that was really caused by horse or cattle traffic, and cries from bikers about those "kamikaze" riders who through their antics threaten to close even more trails to all of us.

The authors of this series have been very careful to guide you to only those trails that are open to mountain biking (or at least were open at the time of their research), and without exception have warned of the damage done to our sport through injudicious riding. My personal views on this matter appear in the Afterword, but all of us can benefit from glancing over the following International Mountain Bicycling Association (IMBA) Rules of the Trail before saddling up.

1. *Ride on open trails only.* Respect trail and road closures (ask if not sure), avoid possible trespass on private land, obtain permits and authorization as may be required. Federal and State wilderness areas are closed to cycling.

2. *Leave no trace.* Be sensitive to the dirt beneath you. Even on open trails, you should not ride under conditions where you will leave evidence of your passing, such as on certain soils shortly after rain. Observe the different types of soils and trail construction; practice low-impact cycling. This also means staying on the trail and not creating any new ones. Be sure to pack out at least as much as you pack in.

3. *Control your bicycle!* Inattention for even a second can cause disaster. Excessive speed can maim and threaten people; there is no excuse for it!

4. *Always yield the trail.* Make known your approach well in advance. A friendly greeting (or a bell) is considerate and works well; startling someone may cause loss of trail access. Show your respect when passing others by slowing to a walk or even stopping. Anticipate that other trail users may be around corners or in blind spots.

5. *Never spook animals.* All animals are startled by an unannounced approach, a sudden movement, or a loud noise. This can be dangerous for you, for others, and for the animals. Give animals extra room and time to adjust to you. In passing, use special care and follow the directions of horseback riders (ask if uncertain). Running cattle and disturbing wild animals is a serious offense. Leave gates as you found them, or as marked.

6. *Plan ahead.* Know your equipment, your ability, and the area in which you are riding—and prepare accordingly. Be self-sufficient at all times. Wear a helmet, keep your machine in good condition, and carry necessary supplies for changes in weather or other conditions. A well-executed trip is a satisfaction to you and not a burden or offense to others.

For more information, contact IMBA, P.O. Box 412043, Los Angeles, CA 90041, (818) 792-8830.

HITTING THE TRAIL

Once again, because this is a "where-to," not a "how-to" guide, the following will be brief. If you're a veteran trail rider these suggestions might serve to remind you of something you've forgotten to pack. If you're a newcomer, they might convince you to think twice before hitting the backcountry unprepared.

Water: I've heard the questions dozens of times. "How much is enough? One bottle? Two? Three?! But think of all that extra weight!" Well, one simple physiological fact should convince you to err on the side of excess when it comes to deciding how much water to pack: a human working hard in 90-degree temperature needs approximately ten quarts of fluids every day. Ten quarts. That's two and a half gallons—12 large water bottles, or 16 small ones. And, with water weighing in at approximately 8 pounds per gallon, a one-day supply comes to a whopping 20 pounds.

In other words, pack along two or three bottles even for short rides. And make sure you can purify the water found along the trail on longer routes. When writing of those routes where this could be of critical importance, each author has provided information on where water can be found near the trail—if it can be found at all. But drink it untreated and you run the risk of disease. (See *Giardia* in the Glossary.)

One sure way to kill both the bacteria and viruses in water is to boil it for ten minutes, plus one minute more for each 1,000 feet of elevation above sea level. Right. That's just how you want to spend your time on a bike ride. Besides, who wants to carry a stove, or denude the countryside stoking bonfires to boil water?

Luckily, there is a better way. Many riders pack along the effective, inexpensive, and only slightly distasteful tetraglycine hydroperiodide tablets (sold under the names Potable Aqua, Globaline, and Coughlan's, among others). Some invest in portable, lightweight purifiers that filter out the crud. Yes, purifying water with tablets or filters is a bother. But catch a case of Giardia sometime and you'll understand why it's worth the trouble.

Tools: Ever since my first cross-country tour in 1965 I've been kidded about the number of tools I pack on the trail. And so I will exit entirely from this discussion by providing a list compiled by two mechanic (and mountain biker) friends of mine. After all, since they make their livings fixing bikes, and get their kicks by riding them, who could be a better source?

These two suggest the following as an absolute minimum:

> tire levers
> spare tube and patch kit
> air pump
> allen wrenches (3, 4, 5, and 6 mm)
> six-inch crescent (adjustable-end) wrench
> small flat-blade screwdriver
> chain rivet tool
> spoke wrench

But, while they're on the trail, their personal tool pouches contain these additional items:

> channel locks (small)
> air gauge
> tire valve cap (the metal kind, with a valve-stem remover)
> baling wire (ten or so inches, for temporary repairs)

duct tape (small roll for temporary repairs or tire boot)
boot material (small piece of old tire or a large tube patch)
spare chain link
rear derailleur pulley
spare nuts and bolts
paper towel and tube of waterless hand cleaner

First-Aid Kit: My personal kit contains the following, sealed inside double Ziploc bags:

sunscreen
aspirin
butterfly-closure bandages
Band-Aids
gauze compress pads (a half-dozen 4" x 4")
gauze (one roll)
ace bandages or Spenco joint wraps
Benadryl (an antihistamine, in case of allergic reactions)
water purification tablets
Moleskin / Spenco "Second Skin"
hydrogen peroxide, iodine, or Mercurochrome (some kind of antiseptic)
snakebite kit

Final Considerations: The authors of this series have done a good job in suggesting that specific items be packed for certain trails—raingear in particular seasons, a hat and gloves for mountain passes, or shades for desert jaunts. Heed their warnings, and think ahead. Good luck.

Dennis Coello
St. Louis

OHIO

Northern Ohio

When the Industrial Age swept the United States, it was Lake Erie that helped change Ohio's future from a rural agricultural state to a highly urbanized one. Nowhere is the industrial base more evident than along northern Ohio's lake-front. From Toledo in the west, where mills and factories emerged along the Maumee River, to Cleveland in the east, where steel production is renowned, northern Ohio is an icon of American industry. Even so, you can find places to mountain bike, and interestingly enough, some of the more popular places to ride are not there *in spite of* the industry but *because* of it.

Take the Miami and Erie Canal Towpath Trail along the Maumee River, for instance. Beginning in the 1800s, the canal was a vital part of the transportation system that helped industrialize this area. The Castalia Quarry opened for business near Sandusky in the 1870s and supplied limestone to the region on and off again until 1965. Now it serves as a reserve area and is a popular riding place for the Sandusky Bicycle Club. Finally, the Ohio and Erie Canal helped make Akron and Cleveland the cities they are today. The towpath trail in the heart of the Cuyahoga Valley National Recreation Area gives mountain bikers a quiet, comfortable place to ride.

Northern Ohio is also home to the Resthaven Wildlife Area outside of Sandusky, which was known as the "Castalia prairie" before it was mined. The riding is easy here, but things can get a little more challenging as you head over to Hinkley Reservation and Findley State Park. Neither area presents insurmountable challenges, and you'll find that the riding is fun. Finally, the southernmost ride in this part of the state is at Alum Creek State Park just north of Columbus, where local mountain bikers have succeeded in getting a section of the park set aside for mountain bike use.

Another path referenced in the Findley State Park chapter and several of the other Ohio chapters is the Buckeye Trail. The Buckeye Trail does not officially appear in this guide, but it's worth mentioning. This trail connects the four corners of Ohio with over 1,200 miles of hiking trails and travels through more than 40 of the state's 88 counties. It follows everything from old canal towpaths and abandoned right-of-ways to farmlands, forests, parks, and urban areas. While this is primarily a hiking trail, certain sections are open to mountain bikes—mostly, those sections that travel over public roads or through parks and forests already permitting bicycle use. For more information, write:

Buckeye Trail Association, Inc.
P.O. Box 254
Worthington, OH 43085

The trail descriptions that follow were written with the help of several people. Thanks to Tom Striggow for information about the Miami and Erie Towpath Trail, Amy Grubbe for help with the Castalia Quarry Reserve and Resthaven Wildlife Area, Lou Vetter for input on Findley State Park and Hinckley Reservation, and Dan Negley for information about Alum Creek State Park.

RIDE 1 *MIAMI AND ERIE CANAL TOWPATH TRAIL*

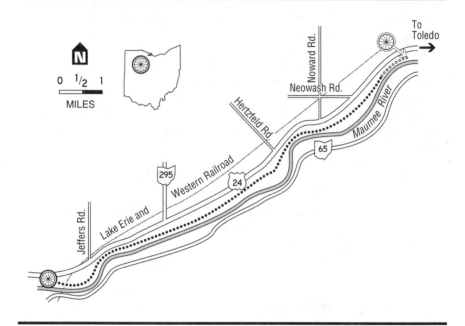

RIDE 1 *MIAMI AND ERIE CANAL TOWPATH TRAIL*

Riders of all ages and abilities will enjoy their ride down the remnants of the Miami and Erie Canal towpath. This 8-mile one-way (16 miles total) out-and-back takes you from Providence Metropark to Farnsworth Metropark. Your impression of Toledo may be of industry, but this ride will change your mind. This dirt and stone double-track follows the Maumee River, affording many views of the waterway. The canal itself is being restored to operating condition.

Just east of the Providence trailhead is the Ludwig Mill. Built in 1864, the mill has an operating grain and saw mill replete with a working waterwheel. The structure also serves as an interpretative center with displays and demonstrations.

Spring is especially scenic here when wildflowers, dogwoods, and red bud trees are in bloom. Return in the fall to see the brilliant yellow leaves of the sugar maples. Make sure you stop at Bend View for a panoramic sight of the Maumee River. Aside from the deer, red fox, and weasel, you might be lucky enough to see an osprey or a migratory bald eagle.

General location: The trail runs between Grand Rapids and Waterville.
Elevation change: The terrain is flat, and the riding is easy.
Season: The trail is off-limits to bikes from January through March because of soft soil conditions.
Services: Water and rest rooms are available at the trailheads and at Bend View Metropark. All services are available in Maumee and Toledo.
Hazards: Since the trail is popular, watch out for other trail users.
Rescue index: There are phones at both trailheads. You should find other users on the trail. Also, you're never far from US 24 if you need to flag someone down.
Land status: Toledo Metroparks.
Maps: Write Toledo Metroparks at the address below for maps of Providence and Farnsworth Metroparks.
Finding the trail: Providence trailhead: From Interstate 80, take Exit 4, Reynolds Road. Go south on Reynolds Road, which becomes Conant Road, for about 4 miles. At the second light, turn right onto US 24 and in roughly 15 miles you will see the main entrance. To get to the trailhead, head toward the river. You can't miss it.

On the way to the Providence trailhead, you'll encounter Farnsworth Park about 1 mile after you pass OH 64.

Sources of additional information:

Metropark District
Administrative Offices
5100 West Central Avenue
Toledo, OH 43615
(419) 535-3050

Notes on the trail: The trail is blazed in blue and easy to follow.

RIDE 2 *CASTALIA QUARRY RESERVE*

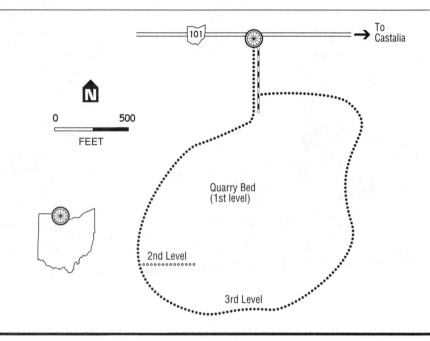

RIDE 2 *CASTALIA QUARRY RESERVE*

Why include a mountain bike trail only two miles long? Because it's a two-mile stretch that you're not likely to find anywhere else. This trail circles the Castalia Quarry Reserve, a quarry site active from the late 1870s to the 1960s. In fact, you can extend your trip by riding directly inside the quarry bed. You won't need a lot of stamina for this ride, even though one spot on the trail is the point of highest elevation in Erie County. (Remember, this is northern Ohio.) From there, you'll be able to look out onto Lake Erie and catch a glimpse of South Bass Island. You may also see the granite column of Perry's Victory and International Peace on the island. The trail is wide, and while you wouldn't want to take a shortcut into the quarry bed from the rim, you're still pretty safe from the edge. It's not fenced off, though, and you'll want to know how to ride a bike, or at least know where your brakes are.

Feel free just to tool around in the quarry bed, but stay out of the sand dunes (due to park regulations). Riding in the quarry is a unique experience. Because

Amy pedals the trail around Castalia Quarry Reserve before heading into the quarry bed.

it's more open, the quarry bed is windier than the rest of the area. So on days when it's normally cold and windy—well, don't open an umbrella. You'll need stronger technical skills because of the loose gravel and exposed limestone here. This is a great little trail to ride. If you're having fun on that family vacation out at Cedar Point Amusement Park in Sandusky, continue the fun at Castalia.

General location: One mile west of Castalia, off OH 101, about six miles southeast of Sandusky.

Elevation change: The climb along the quarry is gradual, and the overall elevation change is minor.

Season: Any time. Winter can be windy down in the quarry bed. After a rain, the trail dries out quickly because of its loam and sand base, but if you ride when it's wet, it's like going through glue.

Services: Bring your own water. Castalia has a few food shops. Sandusky has all services.

Hazards: Don't ride too close to the edge—stay on the designated trail.

Rescue index: You're never far from OH 101, where you can flag down a motorist.

Land status: Erie Metroparks. In order to ride alone here, you will need to take a riding test from the Sandusky Bicycle Club and fill out a permit application from Erie Metroparks; this is part of an arrangement the club has to keep the area open for mountain bikes. The test involves riding the trail with a member of the club who will point out the dangers to you. Let's follow the rules and not lose the privilege.

Maps: The map in this book may be as good as it gets, although you can look at the USGS 7.5 minute quad for Castalia.

Finding the trail: From the Interstate 80/90 Ohio Turnpike, take Exit 7, OH 250. Go north on OH 250 for 5.5 miles to OH 2. Take OH 2 west for 5.5 miles to OH 101 and go south for 4.5 miles, at which point you'll see a sign for Castalia Quarry Reserve. Park there on the right side of the road. The trailhead entrance is on the other side of OH 101.

Sources of additional information:

> Erie Metroparks
> 3910 East Perkins Ave
> Huron, OH 44839
> (419) 625-7783

Notes on the trail: From the trailhead, ride up a short hill and curve to your right. If you go straight, you enter the quarry bed. There are three elevation levels. The first is the quarry bed itself. Then there's a second level at the back of the quarry, accessible from the northwest edge of the main trail; you can ride to the dead end and glimpse the bed below and the upper rim above. The third level is the main trail itself that circles the outer rim of the quarry.

Resthaven Wildlife Area is on the other side of OH 101.

RIDE 3   *RESTHAVEN WILDLIFE AREA*

Resthaven Wildlife Area is a beautiful spot filled with woodlands, grasslands, and numerous ponds. While the 2,272-acre area is designated for hunting and fishing, folks in the Sandusky Bicycle Club like to come here to do a little off-road riding as well. Round trip, there are about 6 miles (12 miles total) of out-and-back gravel roads, but you can make this ride much longer by adding the grass trail loops that encompass many of the ponds. Traveling down the gravel roads is easy, and there is almost no elevation change. Taking the grass spurs is not too difficult, just a little jarring (this section is affectionately called Paris-Roubaix by members of the Sandusky Bicycle Club). If you bring your fishing pole with you, expect to catch largemouth bass, northern pike, channel catfish, and other game fish. Above-water wildlife includes pheasant, raccoons, woodchucks, rail, woodcock, and gallinules. You'll also find prairie plants like big bluestem, little bluestem, Indian grass, and prairie dock. In short, the whole family will enjoy a pleasant ride, and the more adventurous will tackle "Paris-Roubaix."

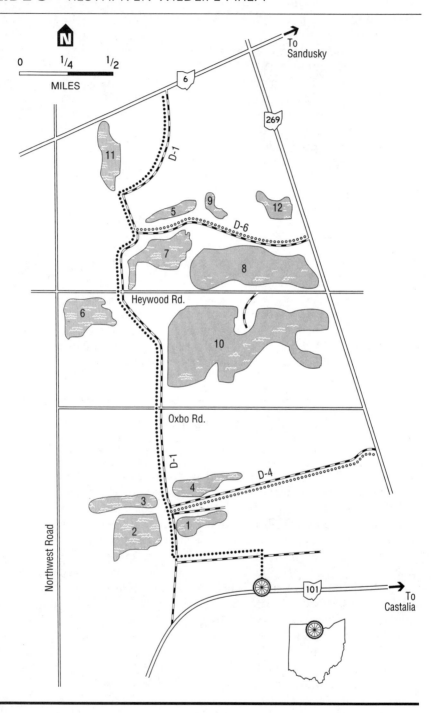

Amy tackles "Paris-Roubaix" around one of Resthaven's ponds.

General location: A mile west of Castalia, off OH 101, about 6 miles southeast of Sandusky.

Elevation change: Negligible.

Season: The grass trails can be overgrown in the summer. The interior access roads may be closed from the opening of hunting season in the fall until after the spring thaw, so you might want to check on availability with the wildlife manager at the address below.

Services: Bring your own water. Castalia has a few food shops. Sandusky has all services.

Hazards: Watch out for hunters and hikers. You may run into an occasional pothole on the gravel roads.

Rescue index: You can flag down traffic on OH 101 on the south side of Resthaven, OH 6 on the north side, and OH 269 on the east side. You may find less traffic on Northwest Road on the west side of Resthaven, and on Heywood Road and Oxbo Road, which cut through the center of the area.

Land status: Ohio Department of Natural Resources—Division of Wildlife.

Maps: You can get a map of Resthaven from the Ohio DNR. The USGS 7.5 minute quad for this area is Castalia.

Finding the trail: From the Interstate 80/90 Ohio Turnpike, take Exit 7, OH 250. Take OH 250 north 5.5 miles to OH 2. Take OH 2 west 5.5 miles to OH 101. Go south on OH 101 for 4.5 miles and you'll see a sign for Castalia Quarry

Reserve. Park there on the right side of the road. You can begin your ride from the back of the parking lot.

Sources of additional information:

> Resthaven Wildlife Area Manager
> Box 155
> Castalia, OH 44824
> (419) 684-5049

> Wildlife District Two Office
> 952 Lima Avenue
> Box A
> Findley, OH 45840
> (419) 424-5000

Notes on the trail: From the rear of the parking lot, go straight back on a single-track trail that will swing slightly to the left. In a few yards, you'll come to a narrow, private gravel road. Go left on that road for half a mile until you run into Herr Road. Turn right on Herr, which will take you into Resthaven. (You can also ride up OH 101 to Herr Road, too.)

Your main out-and-back follows the gravel road, D-1. You might also explore other gravel roads such as D-4 and D-6, which are bordered by several ponds. Get out and explore the grass trails, too. Ponds 10 and 2 have nice grass trails circling them. In essence, if you see a grass trail that looks friendly, check it out!

Castalia Quarry Reserve is just on the other side of OH 101.

RIDE 4 *FINDLEY STATE PARK*

There are over ten miles of trails to explore at Findley State Park, which essentially forms a loop around Findley Lake. The dirt single-track trails are wide because they were originally used as logging roads when the area was a state forest. The section of the Buckeye Trail that runs through the park is narrower than the other trails and has more roots and rocks. It's also steeper, with a 35- to 45-degree downgrade. Most trails, though, will be easy enough for everyday cyclists. You'll even find a couple of stream crossings, and you'll ride along several ravines on the Hickory Grove Trail. The wooded area along this trail is the most natural; many of the other trails have more recent growth.

At Findley State Park, you'll find red maple, white ash, wild black cherry, and red pine in this second growth forest, as well as wildflowers like spring beauties, Dutchman's-breeches, trillium, and bloodroot. You'll likely see deer, red

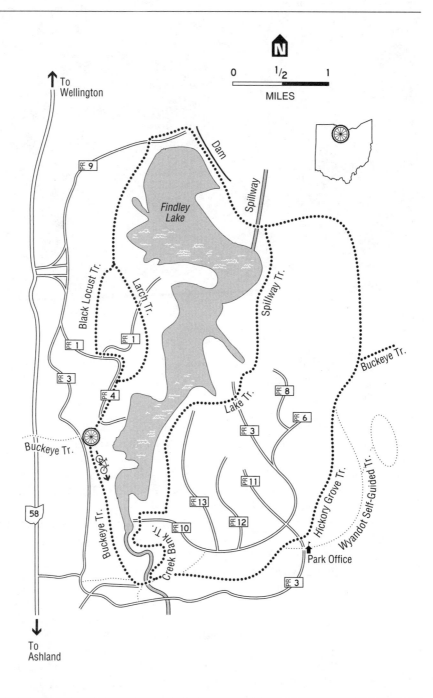

To
Wellington

N

0   1/2   1
MILES

Dam

Spillway

Findley
Lake

Black Locust Tr.

Larch Tr.

PR 9

PR 1

PR 1

PR 3

PR 4

Spillway Tr.

Buckeye Tr.

Lake Tr.

PR 8

PR 6

PR 3

Buckeye Tr.

58

Buckeye Tr.

Creek Bank Tr.

PR 11

PR 13

PR 10

PR 12

Hickory Grove Tr.

Wyandot Self-Guided Tr.

Park Office

PR 3

To
Ashland

At Findley State Park, keep your eyes peeled for the Duke's skipper butterfly, but at this spot, keep your eye on the old wooden bridge.

fox, and even migratory ospreys and hawks. And this park has a sanctuary for the Duke's skipper butterfly. If you're lucky, perhaps you'll spot one of these rare insects.

General location: Off OH 58, 2 miles south of Wellington.
Elevation change: At 980 feet above sea level, the elevation change is only about 50 feet.
Season: Since this is a sensitive area and hikers get first priority, the winter is best; the cooler weather keeps down the number of hikers. Do what you can to avoid any conflicts—don't wreck it for everybody.
Services: Water and camping are available in the state park. Oberlin has all services.
Hazards: Since the area is popular, watch out for hikers.
Rescue index: There is usually someone available at the camp check-in station.
Land status: Ohio state park.
Maps: The state park has a good map showing the trails. Pick one up at the check-in station or write to the park at the address below. The USGS 7.5 minute quad covering most of the area is Wellington. The southernmost section falls into Sullivan.
Finding the trail: From Interstate 80/90, the Ohio Turnpike, take Exit 8, OH 57. Take OH 57 south for half a mile to OH 113. Go west on OH 113 for 5.2

miles to OH 58. Then go south on OH 58 for 16 miles. The entrance to Findley State Park will be on your left. As you pull in, curve to the right and follow Park Road 3 to the Picnic Pines parking area.

Sources of additional information:

Findley State Park
25381 State Road 58
Wellington, OH 44090-9208
(216) 647-4490

Notes on the trail: You can begin the ride on the Buckeye Trail (also called Hickory Grove Trail), which you'll see through the trees on the south side of the parking lot. If you ride instead through a clearing at the opposite end of the lot, you'll cross over a rickety bridge and out onto another parking lot. At the other end of that lot, you can pick up the Larch Trail and head that way. Or feel free to start your ride from any other parking area.

You can make a wide or narrow loop around the lake, depending on which trail you choose. The Spillway Trail is smooth and cuts closer to the lake. Further out is the Hickory Grove Trail, where you'll find the ravines and stream crossings. Also, the Buckeye Trail, which runs parallel to the Creekbank Trail, is fairly steep. You may have to portage here.

There is some confusion about Findley State Park's accessibility to mountain bikes. You might wish to confirm this before you ride.

RIDE 5 *HINCKLEY RESERVATION*

Let Capistrano keep its swallows. Hinckley Reservation has its buzzards. (More on that later.) The trail at Hinckley Reservation, roughly five miles long, makes a circular loop on old logging roads, gravel paths, dirt single-track, and the bridle path. You won't gain much speed through most of the ride, but you're guaranteed a workout crossing over boulders and deadfall, and tackling several short climbs and descents. You'll ride through sections of pine, hardwoods, meadows, and around a man-made lake. If you choose, you can ride along Nelson Ledges, the base of the cliffs where the earth shifted centuries ago, creating several small caves the size of bathroom stalls. The base of the cliffs is fairly rocky, so expect to get off and portage.

The beginning of the ride along an old road is easy, but the trail grows more difficult as you go further. You'll need moderate technical skills as you ride close to nature, seeing the forest from the inside: gorges, lakes, underbrush, and a few stream crossings. In fact, you'll probably want to carry your bike through the streams because the crossings are steep. No panoramic vistas on this ride, but

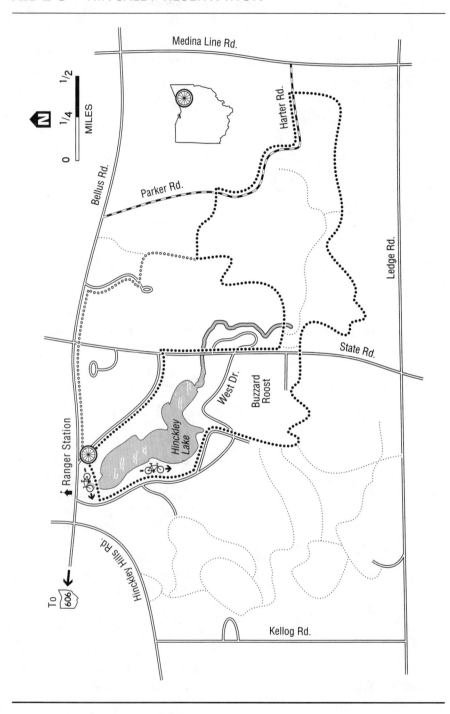

you will get to see several fascinating stone carvings near Worden's Ledges. The sandstone carvings include a clipper ship, a sphinx, a bible, a cross, and a face. Stop for a better look.

Now, about the buzzards. Every March 15, the buzzards return to Hinckley Reservation, where they have been coming since before the turn of the century. As legend has it, back in the 1800s the local people wanted to get rid of all the wild animals in the area, so hunters formed a circle around the woods and walked to the center, killing everything in their path. They piled up the carcasses, which attracted the buzzards. Every year since, the birds have returned in search of another free meal. It may not be a pretty story, but it is compelling.

General location: About 20 miles south of Cleveland.

Elevation change: While there isn't more than 50 feet of overall gain and the short climbs don't sound like a lot, ride in and out of 15 gorges and you'll feel the elevation.

Season: Winter riding is best because the summer attracts many insects and riding through the sticker bushes isn't fun either. Also, the weekend around March 15 gets quite busy as visitors from miles around come out to see the buzzards return.

Services: Bring your own water. There is a concession stand open in the summer by the swimming area. Hinckley, Cleveland, and several of the surrounding suburbs have all services.

Hazards: Be careful riding along the top of the cliffs. There are no guardrails and you won't like the 90-degree drop of 20 to 30 feet. Ouch. You don't have to ride up the cliffs, though; you can take a path around them.

Rescue index: You're never more than a half mile from civilization at any point on the trail.

Land status: Cleveland Metroparks.

Maps: The USGS 7.5 minute quad is West Richfield.

Finding the trail: From the Ohio Turnpike, take Interstate 71 south for approximately 10 miles. Get off at OH 303 and take that east roughly 12 miles. Go through Hinckley and south on OH 606 for about 4 miles to Bellus Road. Turn left on Bellus and follow the signs. You'll see a small ranger station on your left and a dam on your right. Turn right on the first road after the dam. You'll see the entrance a few yards ahead. Park by the concession stand.

Sources of additional information:

Cleveland Metroparks
4101 Fulton Parkway
Cleveland, OH 44144-1923
(216) 351-6300

Notes on the trail: Pass the concession stand to begin your ride. Cross a footbridge and ride across the grass to the west point of the dam. From there, pick up the multi-purpose trail running parallel to the paved road. Turn right onto the logging road where the paved road takes a hairpin turn and starts to climb up.

Hinckley Reservation is the pendant on what is referred to as the "Emerald Necklace," the system of reservations circling Cleveland. Several of the Metropark facilities contain all-purpose trails. Contact Cleveland Metroparks for more information.

RIDE 6   OHIO AND ERIE CANAL TOWPATH TRAIL

This 20-mile each way (40 miles total) out-and-back trail follows the remnants of the Ohio and Erie Canal, located in the Cuyahoga Valley National Recreation Area. The trail is limestone gravel and flat, making this a very easy ride for the entire family. There's much to see along the towpath route, including old houses, cornfields, meadows, marshes, and woods. You'll observe several locks and aqueducts, and even an operating old-time lock near Independence by the Canal Visitor Center. Your ride often parallels the Valley Railroad tracks and the Cuyahoga River. The canal is dry in spots, but contains more water north of Peninsula. You might want to get off your bike and visit Deep Lock Quarry, a former sandstone quarry and the site of the remains of the deepest lock on the canal. If you're more interested in natural construction projects, you'll find a beaver dam south of Peninsula.

It would be your loss if you came to the Cuyahoga Valley National Recreation Area and only rode the towpath. The Canal Visitor Center contains exhibits on the history of the park. Several historical places are worth seeing as well: Wilson's Mill, the last operating mill on the canal; Hale Farm, a restored brick farmstead belonging to one of the earliest settlers in the area; and across the street from the farm, a restored village containing blacksmiths, potters, weavers, candlemakers, and their crafts. The old canal town of Peninsula is another popular tourist area filled with shops and restaurants. In the summer, you might consider spending an evening at the Blossom Music Center, listening to the Cleveland Orchestra under the stars. If you're a theater buff, you might attend summer stock at the Porthouse Theater. There are also several parks within Cuyahoga Valley where you can hike rock ledges and waterfalls, swim, golf, cross-country ski, downhill ski, and sled. There are plenty of attractions to keep you entertained no matter what time of year you come.

General location: Eight miles south of Cleveland.
Elevation change: Negligible.
Season: Enjoy this trail all year long; it's fun any time.
Services: The town of Peninsula has all services, as do Cleveland and Akron.

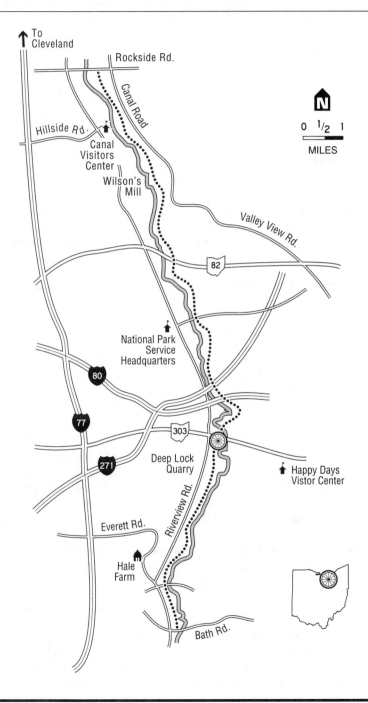

Hazards: Proceed with caution on some bridges and on the boardwalk when it's freezing. Keep an eye out for other bikers, joggers, and hikers on this popular trail.

Rescue index: The trail is heavily used, so encountering other people won't be a problem.

Land status: National Park Service.

Maps: The Cuyahoga Valley Recreation Area will send you a map of the area and its attractions. Write them at the address below. The USGS 7.5 minute quads are Northfield and Peninsula.

Finding the trail: From the intersection of Interstate 80 and OH 21, go south on OH 21 about 1.5 miles to I-77. Take I-77 south for about 3 miles to I-271. Then take I-271 north for 3.5 miles to OH 303, and take OH 303 for about 2 miles to Peninsula. In Peninsula, turn left at the traffic light by Fisher's Restaurant. Go one block and turn left again. You'll see the parking area for the trail and signs directing you to the trailhead.

Contact Cuyahoga Valley National Recreation Area for additional places to pick up the trail.

Sources of additional information:

Cuyahoga Valley National Recreation Area
15610 Vaughn Road
Brecksville, OH 44141-3097
(216) 526-5256

Happy Days Visitor Center
(800) 257-9477 (local calls only)
Canal Visitor Center
(800) 445-9667 (local calls only)

Notes on the trail: Peninsula isn't at either end of the towpath, but this is a good place to start because of the convenient parking, restaurants, shops, and other services. Let the bike riders hit the trails. The others can hit the shops.

The trail endpoints are at Rockside Road and Bath Road, but plans are underway to extend the trail in both directions.

RIDE 7 ALUM CREEK STATE PARK MOUNTAIN BIKE TRAIL

The military once used this area for practicing tank maneuvers. You'll be able to make some maneuvers here too as you ride the narrow single-track trails. Officials at Alum Creek State Park, working in conjunction with local bike shops who helped with fund-raising for the parking lot and signage, have developed a two-part trail. There's a four-mile loop designed for beginning riders and

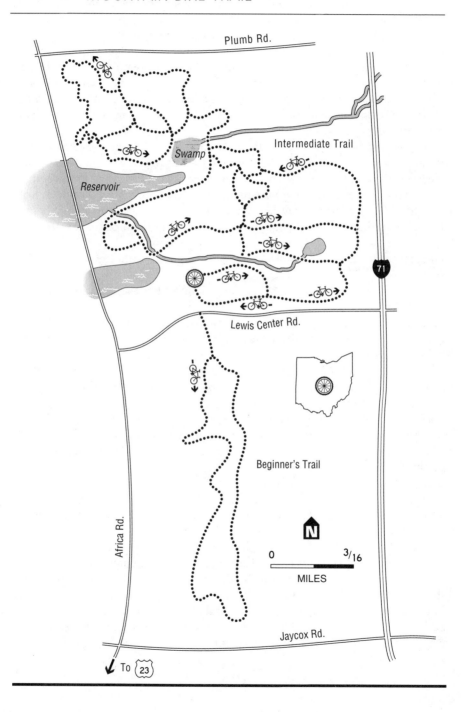

a five-mile connecting loop for intermediate riders. The trail resembles what Dan Negley, manager of Break Away Cycling and Fitness, rode in his home town. "This reminds me of back where I'm from in Nebraska down by the river—single-track trails with lots of curves and overgrowth."

You'll like testing your skills on the winding trails. There are no serious switchbacks, but ruts, roots, stumps, ditches, and a stream crossing will challenge you without being too menacing. The bridge crossings can be tricky, as some of them are little more than branches laid across ditches. Advanced riders can depart from the main trail and tackle the user-made spurs, which are steeper and rockier.

Among the highlights is a ridge that runs along a ravine overlooking a swampy area at the tip of a cove. On one part of the ridge, you'll take a fast curve down and, before you know it, you're on a tricky bridge followed by a few ditches. If you take one user-made trail, you can visit a wonderful old "carpeted" tree, hollowed out like Winnie-the-Pooh's house and probably used by hunters. I didn't see Pooh, but you will find deer, groundhogs, and waterfowl.

General location: Twelve miles north of Columbus from the Interstate 270 beltway.

Elevation change: You'll find a few minor climbs, but the elevation change is not great.

Season: The best time to ride is in the winter since the trail is more heavily traveled in the summer. Also, from May to late summer, you may be besieged by ticks and poison ivy.

Services: You can camp at Alum Creek State Park. All services are available in Delaware and, of course, Columbus. For bike service, try Break Away Cycling and Fitness in Delaware.

Hazards: Look for stumps, roots, and a few tricky bridge crossings.

Rescue index: The area is basically a square mile surrounded by roads. Therefore, you're never more than a half mile from a road. There is a park office on the east side of the lake.

Land status: State park.

Maps: Alum Creek State Park has a map of the entire park, but the current mountain bike trail is not too detailed on it. The state park is working on a more detailed map. The USGS 7.5 minute quad is Galena.

Finding the trail: From the I-270 Beltway north of Columbus, take US 23 north for 6 miles to Lewis Center Road. Turn right on Lewis Center Road and go 4.5 miles to the 4-way stop at Africa Road. Turn left onto Africa Road and go a short distance until Lewis Center Road picks up again. Turn right on Lewis Center Road and follow that for a half mile to the sign for Alum Creek State Park Mountain Bike Trail. The 5-mile connecting loop begins at the end of the parking area. The 4-mile trail is on the other side of the road.

Dan whizzes through the single-track at Alum Creek State Park, one of only a handful of exclusive mountain bike trails.

Sources of additional information:

Alum Creek State Park
3615 South Old State Road
Delaware, OH 43015
(614) 548-4631

Break Away Cycling and Fitness
81 East William Street
Delaware, OH 43015
(614) 363-3232

Notes on the trail: The main trail is marked, but feel free to explore the user-made spurs and dead ends. If you get turned around, listen for the traffic on I-71 and head in that direction. Then you can walk north or south to the first road.

Southwestern Ohio

Southwestern Ohio is not exactly a hotbed of mountain biking activity, but it is home to several great recreational sites—Kings Island Amusement Park and a water slide park among them. The two rides listed in this section are just up the road from Cincinnati. Okay, perhaps they're as close to Dayton as they are to Cincinnati, but the latter is known for wonderful chili.

The trails highlight two opposite types of riding. The Little Miami Scenic River Trail is a rail-trail conversion offering easy riding in a historical area. Seven miles southeast of Lebanon is Fort Ancient State Memorial, a Hopewell Indian site on a bluff overlooking the Little Miami River. The park surrounds a series of earthen walls ranging in height from 4 to 25 feet. It's worth heading over to Fort Ancient State Memorial to learn more about the Hopewell culture, which was active between 100 B.C. and 500 A.D.

The trail at Caesar Creek State Park is completely different. Here, you'll appreciate the efforts of the Dayton Bicycle Club, which with the cooperation of park officials, has developed a trail system through the woods that will challenge many riders' abilities.

When I first explored Ohio, these were the first two trails I visited. Not far apart in terms of distance, but polar opposites on the mountain bike chart. Try whichever type of riding grabs you—just make sure you find your way back to Cincinnati for that chili.

RIDE 8   *LITTLE MIAMI SCENIC RIVER TRAIL*

If you like family rides, this multi-purpose trail is perfect for you. This 50-mile each way (100 mile total) out-and-back follows the Little Miami River along an abandoned railroad line. Twenty-two of those miles are paved, and the rest are gravel. This wide trail doesn't require any technical skill. As far as stamina is concerned, travel as many of the miles as you're able. In some spots, the original ballast is rougher than others, but your way will still be passable. You won't be disappointed by the scenery as you meander past farmlands and forests, and occasional gorges and cliffs. The area has historical value as well. Fort Ancient, located on the high bluffs along the river, was built by the Hopewell Indians centuries ago. In addition, Daniel Boone spent a good deal of time along the river. You'll find many songbirds along this trail. (I took great relish as two goldfinches followed me, flitting from branch to branch.) If you're vacationing in the Cincinnati area, consider taking the family here for a relaxing day of riding.

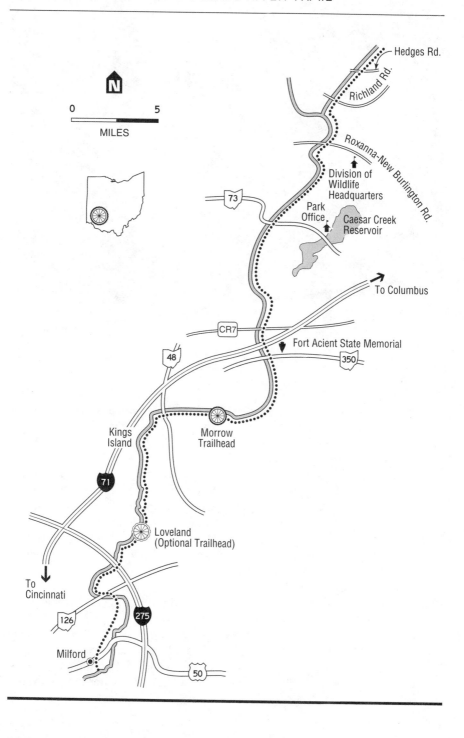

Along this relaxing trail, there's plenty of time to reflect upon the Hopewell Indians, who lived along the Little Miami River.

General location: From Kroger Hill to Spring Valley, following the Little Miami River.

Elevation change: Negligible.

Season: Ride this trail all year long. Spiders spinning their webs across the trail in the summer can be a bit nerve-racking to the faint-hearted.

Services: The trailheads have water, including the Morrow trailhead listed below. Bed-and-breakfasts and motels can be found in Lebanon, Morrow, Loveland, and Milford. I found a quaint shop in Morrow called "Capricorn," which serves refreshments and has a few basic bike essentials. Stop in and talk with the owner. Loveland, on the paved section, has some nice shops and places to eat.

Hazards: Be careful as you cross the street intersections.

Rescue index: The trail passes several towns and houses. You'll find phones at the Loveland and Morrow trailheads.

Land status: Ohio state park.

Maps: The map available from the state park at the address below should meet your needs, as this trail is easy to follow.

Finding the trail: To get to the Morrow trailhead: From Interstate 71, take the Morrow Exit 32, OH 123. Turn right on OH 123 and take that 6 miles into Morrow. When you get to the junctions of OH 123, US 22, and OH 3, turn right at the stoplight onto Pike Street. Go past the next light and turn right on

Center Street. Go barely a block and you will see a grassy area where you can park your car.

Contact Caesar Creek State Park for additional places to pick up the trail.

Sources of additional information:

> Little Miami State Park
> c/o Caesar Creek State Park
> 8570 East State Route 73
> Waynesville, OH 45068-9719
> (513) 897-3055

Notes on the trail: I prefer starting from the Morrow trailhead. This is where the paved section ends and the gravel begins. The mountain biker looking for that relaxing paved ride will ride toward Milford; everyone else will go the other way. You'll find that the gravel section is less traveled than the paved section. If you to choose to ride the entire 50 miles there and back, you can start from either the Milford trailhead in the south or the Hedges Road trailhead (just south of Xenia) in the north.

Begin your ride on the unpaved section out of Morrow, heading north down the paved street from where you parked your vehicle. Cross over a wooden bridge and you'll see the trail splitting off from that.

The Little Miami Scenic Trail is also part of the North Country Trail (see page 64).

RIDE 9   *CAESAR CREEK STATE PARK*

A ranger told me the local mountain bikers were tired of riding on flat terrain—they wanted an area where they could bike-and-hike. Well, they got it here. This trail has some wonderful earthen stairs that I haven't yet figured out how to ride up. This out-and-back trail is 6 miles one way (12 miles total), and you won't be disappointed. Most of the trail is wide dirt single-track with a few grassy sections. The trail is challenging—especially the ups and downs and gullies in the area between Harveysburg Road and Ward Road. The section north of Ward Road is a little flatter, but even it has some steep downhills. Because the climbs and descents aren't long, you can do some fast cranking on this curvy trail, but keep an eye out for roots and rocks. Red-tail hawks, box turtles, and red fox are among the animals you might see in these oak-hickory and beech-maple woodlands.

General location: Northeast of Interstate 71, just outside of Harveysburg.
Elevation change: The climbs and descents are occasionally steep, but the overall elevation change is not significant.

RIDE 9 *CAESAR CREEK STATE PARK*

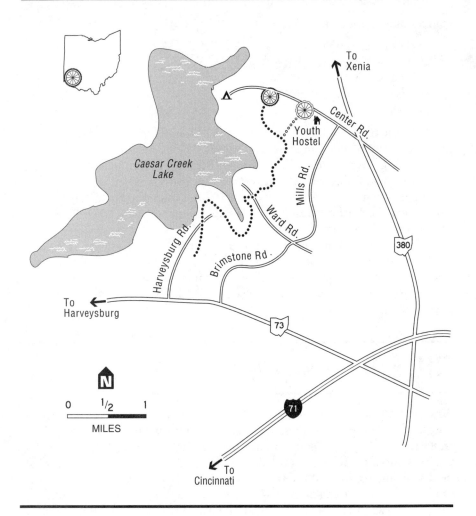

To
Xenia

Center Rd.

Youth
Hostel

Mills Rd.

Caesar Creek
Lake

Ward Rd.

Harveysburg Rd.

Brimstone Rd.

380

To
Harveysburg

73

N

0   ½   1
MILES

71

To
Cincinnati

Season: Any time of year. In the fall, you will enjoy the foliage, but it's also hunting season.

Services: Water is available at the campground. All services are available in Morrow.

Hazards: Be on the lookout for rocks, roots, and other common trail obstacles. Watch out for the occasional hiker as well.

Rescue index: The entrance to the campground is usually staffed. You should also be able to flag down traffic on Ward Road, Brimstone Road, Harveysburg

This single-track is a piece of cake after portaging over the earthen stairs.

Road, and, of course, OH 73. The area is fairly secluded, so ride with a partner.

Land status: State park.

Maps: The USGS 7.5 minute quad for this area is New Burlington.

Finding the trail: From I-71, take Exit 45 for OH 73. Turn right, go about 1 mile to OH 380, and turn left. Go 3 miles to Center Road and turn left again. This will take you directly to the campground where you can park your vehicle.

Sources of additional information:

Caesar Creek State Park
8570 East State Road 73
Waynesville, OH 45068
(513) 897-3055

Notes on the trail: From the campground, ride back to Center Road. Go up Center Road a few yards and you'll see the entrance through the grass on your right. The trail begins on a wide grass path, passing an algae-covered pond. Soon you'll enter the woods and the trail will be signed.

Beware of one tricky spot where the trail enters a clearing with the lake to your right (before Ward Road). Ride uphill in the clearing and you'll find the entrance back into the woods on the side of the clearing around a pumping station.

If you get lost on the trail, head downhill toward the stream, which will take you to Harveysburg Road, Ward Road, or Brimstone Road, depending on where you are.

There is one main trail, but plans are underway to put in spurs around the more difficult sections to accomodate less skilled riders. Check with the park first to verify their access.

Scioto Trail State Forest

Scioto Trail State Forest lies in the lower Scioto Valley. While this area was one of the first regions in Ohio to be settled, the hilly territory where the state forest is located saved it from agricultural development. After the Civil War, though, the area was heavily cut. Now this reforested region is a wonderful gem for some challenging mountain biking. Scioto Trail State Forest, just west of the Scioto River on the Allegheny Plateau, contains some rugged topography. The hills here will test your endurance.

I'll describe two rides at Scioto Trail State Forest. The first takes you on the bridle trail network throughout the forest. On some of these trails, you'll feel as if you're climbing forever, even though it may be only half an hour. The second ride is designed for those who would rather get a workout on the sparsely traveled forest roads—roads with spectacular views of the surrounding hills. Just how sparsely traveled? Time for a story.

After my ride through this area, I drove out on one of the Forest Service roads. As I passed a car on the narrow, freshly laid gravel, I was a little too preoccupied with the scenery. Before I realized it, my van slid off the road and came to rest precariously on the edge of a hill. The slightest movement could have sent the van plunging down the slope. Thank goodness for emergency car phones. In the hour and a half I waited for a tow truck, only two other cars passed me by. These roads are isolated.

RIDE 10   *SCIOTO TRAIL STATE FOREST—BRIDLE TRAILS*

You're not likely to encounter the old tomahawk-carrying hermit who used to live in a cave in this forest—he died over 160 years ago—but you will find over 10 miles of trails available at Scioto Trail State Forest. The various bridle trails are open to mountain bikes, but stay off the hiking trails. Most of the trails are out-and-backs, but if you combine them with the forest roads, you can create loops of varying length, depending upon your own tastes. Every trail will take you back to a road. The dirt trails are wide, but you will find a few obstacles in your path: branches and gullies. But overall, the trails don't require much in the way of technical ability. Your endurance, though, will likely be tapped. Even local mountain bikers consider the trails challenging, and inexperienced riders will walk their bikes quite a bit. There isn't a single trail here that doesn't have a climb. Long Branch, for instance, can be especially tough. For two and a half miles, you'll ride in a relatively flat area along a creek and a ridge, but the last

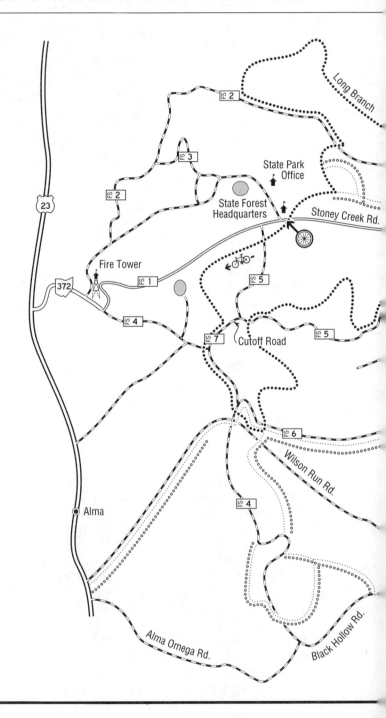

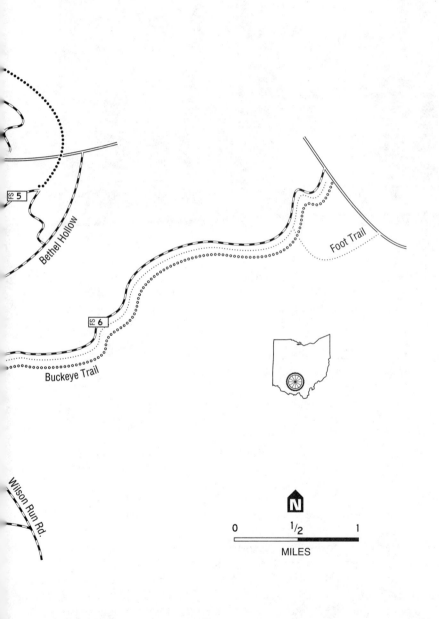

FS 5

Bethel Hollow

FS 6

Buckeye Trail

Foot Trail

Wilson Run Rd.

N

0   1/2   1
MILES

The bridle trails, with little horse traffic, make for a great mountain bike ride.

half mile has a difficult climb. The Headquarters Trail has a lengthy uphill heading into Cutoff Road. Luckily, horses have not rutted the trails too badly since equestrians do not use Scioto Trail State Forest as much as they use other state parks.

General location: Off US 23, 9 miles south of Chillicothe.

Elevation change: There are between 300 and 400 feet of change on the bridle trails.

Season: You can ride here all year, but the fall colors are particularly striking. The spring and the fall are busier, and the spring can be wet. In June, Scioto Trail State Forest hosts a mountain bike campout.

Services: Camping is available. All services can be found in Chillicothe.

Hazards: Besides the usual trail obstacles, watch out for hikers and occasional equestrians.

Rescue index: The Forest Headquarters and the State Park office are usually staffed. The area usually has enough visitors around to provide assistance.

Land status: State forest. There is also a state park contained within the forest boundaries. The trails in the park have recently opened to bicycles.

Maps: You can get a map of the forest from the office and at the fire tower. The USGS 7.5 minute quad for Scioto Trail State Forest is Waverly North.

Finding the trail: From Chillicothe, take US 23 south about 9 miles. At OH 372, you'll see the entrance for Scioto Trail State Forest. Follow the signs to the park office and park there or, if you like, at any of the other parking areas you see. If you park at the office, you can begin your ride on the Headquarters Trail, right off FS 1.

Sources of additional information:

Scioto Trail State Forest
2731 Stoney Creek Road
Chillicothe, OH 45601
(614) 663-2523

Notes on the trail: The trails are marked and easy to follow, so you're not likely to get lost. Stick to the bridle paths. The Buckeye Trail also passes through Scioto Trail State Forest.

RIDE 11 *SCIOTO TRAIL STATE FOREST—FOREST ROAD 2*

If you're visiting Scioto Trail State Forest but you don't wish to ride the bridle trails, do I have an easier scenic ride for you. This route, traveling mostly along Forest Road 2, contains spectacular vistas of the surrounding hills so gorgeous that they should be illegal. Five miles of this eight-and-a-half-mile loop is gravel and fairly isolated. It should take the average rider about an hour and a half to make the trip. Forest Road 2 winds to an elevation of roughly 300 feet before descending near the start of the Cemetery Bridle Trail. This isn't a technical ride, but it may require some endurance on the climb.

Many oaks, especially chestnut oaks, can be found along the ridges, and you may spot wild turkeys as well. If you haven't overdosed on the scenery, be sure to climb to the top of the fire tower for a panoramic picture of the forest.

General location: Off US 23, 9 miles south of Chillicothe.
Elevation change: The elevation change is around 300 feet.
Season: The fall colors in the panoramas you find will delight you.
Services: Camping is available. All services can be found in Chillicothe.
Hazards: Traffic is light on FS 2, so you won't find many hazards.
Rescue index: The Forest Headquarters and the state park office are usually staffed. You may be able to flag down the occasional car on FS 2, but the area is fairly remote.
Land status: State forest.
Maps: You can get a map of the forest from the office and at the fire tower. The USGS 7.5 minute quad for Scioto Trail State Forest is Waverly North.
Finding the trail: From Chillicothe, take US 23 south for about 9 miles. At OH 372, you'll see the entrance for Scioto Trail State Forest. Follow the signs to the park office and park there.

RIDE 11   *SCIOTO TRAIL STATE FOREST /*
FOREST ROAD 2

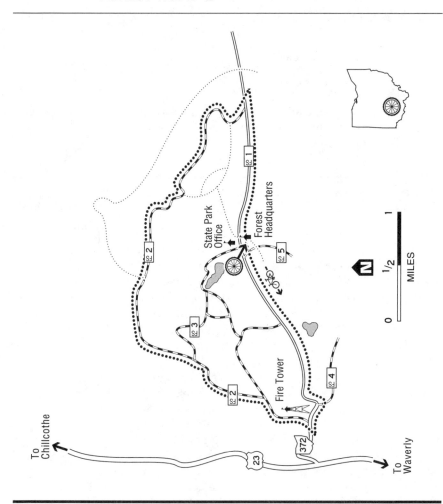

Sources of additional information:

Scioto Trail State Forest
2731 Stoney Creek Road
Chillicothe, OH 45601
(614) 663-2523

Notes on the trail: From the state park headquarters, turn right onto FS 1. This
will intersect with OH 372 in 2 miles. Turn right at the "Forest Headquarters"

Forest Road 2 provides many spectacular views of the hills in southern Ohio.

sign. The gravel starts here, and the fire tower is located by the headquarters. Follow the gravel through the buildings and keep going on the one-way for 1.5 miles. At the intersection of FS 2 and FS 3, take FS 2 for 3.5 miles. When you get to FS 1, turn right and follow that back to your vehicle.

Wayne National Forest— Ironton District

If you want some truly challenging riding, head out to the Ironton District of Wayne National Forest. This national forest consists of two districts and one unit. Each has its own policies regarding mountain bike usage. Here at the Ironton District and at the Athens District, mountain bikes are not permitted on the hiking trails. That's okay. They are permitted on the off-road vehicle (ORV) trails. Trust me. These trails will keep you occupied. Former astronauts John Glenn and Neil Armstrong are from Ohio, and it wouldn't suprise me at all if they both came to the Ironton area to train for the rigors of spaceflight. Hanging Rock will throw steep downhills, moguls, curves, and ruts at you—the whole nine yards. Pine Creek, while a little easier, is still nothing to brush aside. Because of the ORV use, the trails are fast—at least on downhills and straightaways. The uphill climbs are a different matter.

Wayne National Forest, located in southeastern Ohio, is the hilliest region described in this book. Located in the foothills of the Appalachian Mountains, the forest does not have the long, 1,000-plus foot climbs and descents you'll find in central Appalachia, but for those who like to tackle shorter climbs and rapid descents, this is the place.

Another thing you'll appreciate about all three areas of Wayne National Forest is the remoteness. While trails in other parts of the state are populated by various user groups, my mid-week trip to these trails found little use, even by ORVs. This is truly a place of hidden treasures.

RIDE 12 PINE CREEK ORV TRAIL

This 20-mile one-way (40 mile total) out-and-back ORV trail is excellent for those who enjoy cycling on ORV trails but aren't up to the challenges of Hanging Rock. And this trail is good for that beginning hammerhead who wants to hone those technical skills. Similar to Hanging Rock, this trail requires some skills for the moguls, tire ruts, gullies, and loose dirt. The average mountain biker, though, will find this trail doable and will have fun hammering down the hard-packed, wide trail. You'll encounter about six hills to test your endurance. On the trip, you'll see rock ledges and shelters as well as a bridge over Pine Creek.

The trail branches at a Y intersection, and you have your choice of heading to either the Lyra or Wolcott trailhead. Since the climb out of either trailhead is

RIDE 12 *PINE CREEK ORV TRAIL*

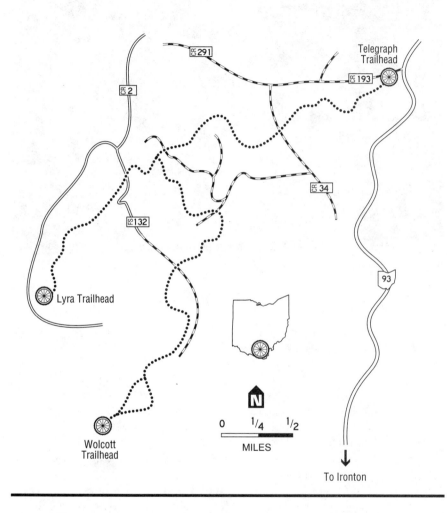

steep, take your choice, but be warned that the Wolcott branch is longer. You'll hit splashes of pine in this otherwise deciduous forest. Also, keep your eyes and ears peeled for wild turkey and the occasional bear. There have been *rare* reports of bears in the area, but consider yourself extremely lucky (or unlucky) if you get the chance to see one.

General location: Wayne National Forest, 22 miles north of Ironton.
Elevation change: The overall elevation change is about 300 feet.

Riding through the pines provides a refreshing change from the moguls and gullies.

Season: The spring and fall colors are pleasing, and the temperatures are more moderate then.

Services: Bring your own water. Camping is available at Lake Vesuvius Recreational Area. Food and lodging are available in Ironton. Huntington, West Virginia has bike service.

Hazards: Look out for ORVs on the trail as well as tire ruts and loose dirt.

Rescue index: This area is isolated and receives few visitors. OH 93 has traffic, but of course the further you ride down the trail, the further away it is.

Land status: Wayne National Forest—Ironton Ranger District.

Maps: The Ironton Ranger District has a map for this trail. Write for one at the address below. The USGS 7.5 minute quads covering this area are Pedro, South Webster, and Gallia for the trailhead.

Finding the trail: From Ironton, take OH 93 north for 23 miles. You'll see a sign for Off Road Vehicle Trailhead—Telegraph. Turn left there onto CR 193 (not identified). Go one-eighth mile and you'll see the parking area on your left. The marked trailhead is on the right side of the parking area.

Sources of additional information:

Ironton Ranger District
Route 2
Box 203
Pedro, OH 45659
(614) 532-3223

Notes on the trail: The trail is marked with brown carsonite signs. However, the Forest Service does have a problem with people vandalizing signs, and there are several user-made trails that might confuse you. Therefore, you might wish to carry a topo map and a compass. Please stick to the designated route and stay off the user-made trails. The area is remote, so don't go alone.

RIDE 13 *HANGING ROCK ORV TRAIL*

There are 26 miles of ORV trails to tackle at Hanging Rock—and "tackle" isn't a strong enough word. I warmed up on Gas Well, one of the easiest trails, enjoying the speed I could attain on the hard-packed trail. But later as I was riding Copperhead, a more difficult trail, I had to stop for a moment to remove my heart from my mouth and put it back where it belongs. The trail contains a steep downhill with several obscene moguls, curves, and ruts. You'll need to borrow technical skills to make it through this area, as it could be dangerous. Ride this only if you know what you're doing! If you're nervous, portage. When you see a sign that says "hill" and shows a curvy arrow, believe it. As you make your way down that hill, somewhere in the back of your mind, you know there's going to be an equally hard uphill. Trust the back of your mind.

Copperhead is just one of the nine trails that blanket the area. Since the trails are designed for ORV use, they are wide and you can pick up speed on many of them. But beware of potholes, ruts made by ORVs, and washouts. Also, this is southern Ohio, so flatlanders take care: you will need to climb hills. Multiple loop options are available to you as the trails connect to one another, so feel free to make a short loop or a long one. There are trails for all ability levels, but most of them are designated "moderate." The trails are well marked and even coded to their difficulty level. Hanging Rock, the trail that gives this area its name, is one of the steepest trails, especially on its west and east ends. As a general rule, as you approach a bridge, expect a downhill followed by an uphill. Where Copperhead leaves High Knob, you'll get a nice view of the river. This is a great area to spend the day. Bring a map and plenty of water, and have at it.

General location: Wayne National Forest, about 10 miles north of Ironton.
Elevation change: You'll experience about 300 feet of elevation change at Hanging Rock.
Season: Late September is a good time because the mornings and evenings are cool, and the days are warm. On weekdays, few people are around, but on weekends, it can get crowded.
Services: Bring your own water. Camping is available at Lake Vesuvius Recreational Area. Food and lodging are available in Ironton. Huntington, West Virginia has bike service.

RIDE 13   *HANGING ROCK ORV TRAIL*

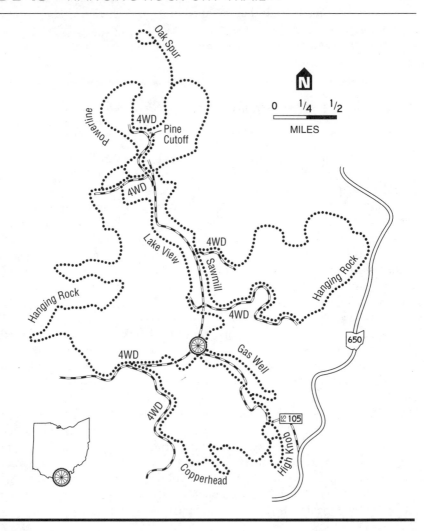

Hazards: Of course, keep an ear out for ORVs. Sections of the trail have potholes, tire ruts, and occasional rocks. Be careful on washouts where the ORVs have torn up the hardpack. Otherwise, you may lose your traction as it's like riding through a patch of sand.

Rescue index: The area is remote. You might pass a rare vehicle on FS 105; OH 650 is busier.

Land status: Wayne National Forest—Ironton Ranger District.

You'll need all your concentration on the fast downhills.

Maps: The Ironton Ranger District has an adequate map of this area. Write to the address below. The USGS 7.5 minute quad is Ironton.

Finding the trail: From US 52 and OH 650 north of Ironton, take OH 650 north for .75 mile. Just before a coal tipple, turn left on FS 105. Go 1.5 miles to the trailhead.

Sources of additional information:

>   Ironton Ranger District
>   Route 2
>   Box 203
>   Pedro, OH 45659
>   (614) 532-3223

Notes on the trail: From the trailhead, you have 2 choices. You can go back up the road a bit to where Gas Well and Hanging Rock cross each other. Start with Gas Well if you like, or with the more difficult Hanging Rock.

Wayne National Forest—
Athens District and Zanesville

The Athens District of Wayne National Forest has only one area open to mountain bikes: Monday Creek Off-Road Vehicle Area. As with the Ironton District, hiking trails are off limits, but Monday Creek, with its over 70 miles of trails, will more than satiate your mountain biking appetite. "Ohio" is Iroquois for "something great," and you'll be muttering "Ohio, Ohio, Ohio!" on these trails. Its reputation as one of the top spots for dirt bike riding in the country should tell you something about what you can expect for our less motorized sport. Monday Creek still has relatively little mountain bike use, while dirt bikers frequently ride in this fabulous area. Unlike the conflicts between equestrian groups and mountain bikers, I haven't found similar tensions with dirt bikers. Obviously, it's a lot easier for a cyclist to hear an oncoming dirt bike than it is for an equestrian to hear a mountain bike. If you want more privacy, stay away on the weekends when the dirt bikers are more prevalent. The area, though, is vast, and you're not likely to meet many other users.

Heading out of Wayne National Forest to the north and east, you'll find several rides for bikers of differing abilities. On the northern border of the forest is Perry Trail Campground, a private campground popular with horses; it will give those beginning and intermediate riders a good experience. Perhaps one of the most challenging areas I've found is a trail on private property south of Zanesville. Zanesville was the hometown of the famous adventure writer, Zane Grey, and riding the trails at Tom Hayes Farm is definitely a thrill. While the trails in the ORV areas are formidable, the narrowness of the trails here tests mountain bikers of all abilities with equal ferociousness.

Not wanting to be responsible for "challenge overload," I'll add that the final trail in this section slows things down a bit. Ohio Power ReCreation Land, a popular fishing and camping area, contains several gravel roads perfect for catching your breath.

Ridden hard or easy, the trails in Wayne National Forest and the Zanesville area offer some of the best mountain biking options in the state.

Thanks to Scott Williams for information about Monday Creek ORV Area, and Dan German for information about Perry Trail Campground and Tom Hayes Farm.

RIDE 14 *MONDAY CREEK ORV AREA*

Serious mountain bikers will love the ORV trails in the Monday Creek area. Scott Williams, the owner of Camp Ohio, puts it succinctly and elegantly when he says, "There are a lot of whoop-de-doos here—some jumps where you can get some air time." Over 70 miles of trails run throughout this area, a whole network of which can be found in the Dorr Run section. The trails are wide and hard-packed, but they are challenging. In fact, *Dirt Wheels*, a major dirt bike magazine, rated this area in the top ten in the nation for dirt bike riding. So imagine what that must mean for mountain bikers! You'll have to match your wits against fallen logs, rocks, moguls, gullies, tire ruts, mud, gas pipelines (don't ride on them), steep climbs, and whatever else Mother Nature can think of to throw at you.

The area has a lot of history and scenery as well. You'll find strip pits off the trail, especially on the Main Corridor. There is a waterfall in the Dorr Run area, but you won't be able to see it from the trail. This region was once home to the world's largest brickyard with the first continuous kiln, and you may find evidence of this on the trails. (I found a few bricks half buried in the dirt here and there.) Off the trail, there are still remants of a kiln south of the New Straitsville area.

If you ride in the winter, you'll get to see some sites off the trail that you can't spot through the summer foliage, including old gas wells, shacks, foundations, sand dug wells, and caves. You may also see steam rising from underground vents.

The three-mile New Straitsville loop is the easiest section, but it gets increasingly difficult as you make your way down the Main Corridor. The most challenging section is Long Ridge, but Snake Hollow and Dorr Run can get complex, too. Dorr Run has steep ridges and good climbs. Monday Creek contains thick forests full of turkey, deer, woodchuck, grouse, and beaver. This area is a good place to spend a few days camping and riding. Carry a topo map and a compass and plan to get lost.

General location: Wayne National Forest, about 15 miles northwest of Athens.
Elevation change: Although the elevation ranges only between 800 and 1,000 feet, the climbs you find are steep.
Season: October, with its fall colors, is a good time to ride. Also, mountain bikers might wish to come out on the weekdays to avoid the many dirt bikers on the weekends.
Services: Bring your own water. You'll find a phone in New Straitsville, and all services are available in Athens. There are two campgrounds off OH 595 near the trails. I found the folks at Camp Ohio to be quite friendly and helpful.

RIDE 14 MONDAY CREEK ORV AREA

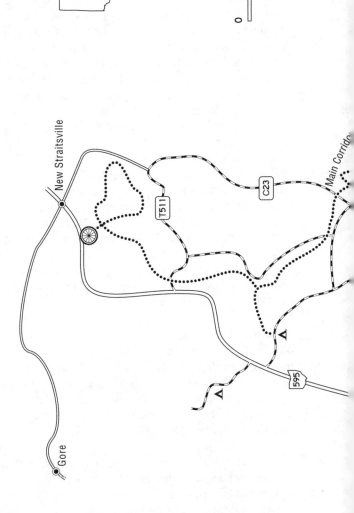

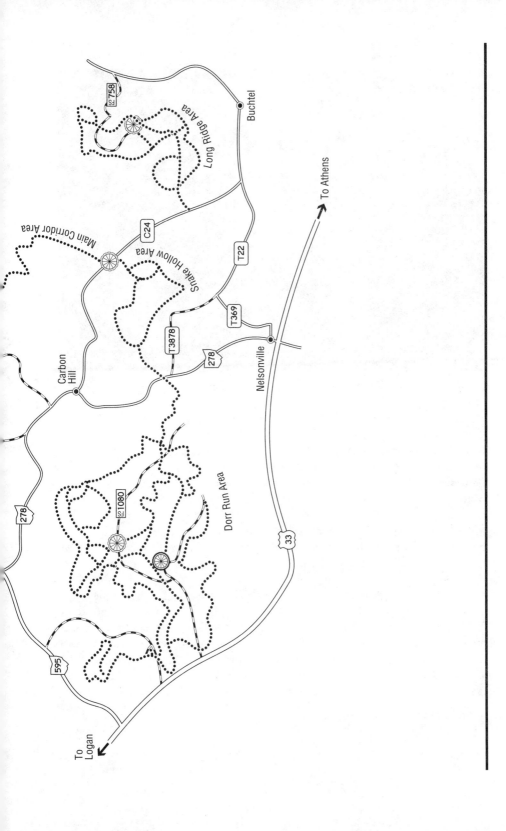

Rock cliffs are one of many fascinating features found at Monday Creek.

Hazards: Look out for the steep climbs, ruts, and other obstacles noted above. Watch out for ORV users, too.

Rescue index: Some of the sections are remote, but you're likely to find traffic on OH 595, OH 278, US 33, and CR 24.

Land status: Wayne National Forest—Athens Ranger District.

Maps: The Athens Ranger District has a map of the area with topographical markings. Write to the address below to get one. The USGS 7.5 minute quads for this area are Gore, New Straitsville, Union Furnace, and Nelsonville.

Finding the trail: For the New Straitsville Trailhead: From US 33, take OH 595 north. Go about 8.5 miles and you'll see the sign for the New Straitsville trailhead. As you begin your ride, you'll see a sign marked "MC" for the Main Corridor. Go a bit further and you'll come to the entrance for the 3-mile loop.

For the Dorr Run Trailhead: At the junction of US 33 and OH 595, go south on US 33 for 1.5 miles. Turn left at the sign for the Dorr Run Trailhead. In 1.3 miles, you'll come to an intersection where you can go straight or branch off to the left. Head straight to the additional parking sign and in another half mile, you'll find a parking area and a sign for the Dorr Run Loop. If you like, you can take the left branch to another parking area.

Sources of additional information:

Athens Ranger District
219 Columbus Road

Athens, OH 45701
(614) 592-6644

Camp Ohio
12063 Gore-Greendale Road
Logan, OH 43138
(614) 753-2303

Notes on the trail: The trails are marked with their level of difficulty. From the Dorr Run trailhead, you can follow the outer perimeter loop marked by brown signs with blue stickers. This will give you a 15-mile ride. Vandals' stealing signs is a problem, so be aware of missing signs. Some of these areas are isolated; ride with a companion.

RIDE 15 *PERRY TRAIL CAMPGROUND*

Beginner and intermediate mountain bikers will like this eleven-mile loop located in the Perry Trail Campground. The single-track and double-track trails form a loop with a few spurs and are wide and well maintained. Consequently, there are only a few ditches and moguls to worry about. The few climbs and descents are not too difficult, especially since the trail surface is smooth. You'll even find one stream crossing, and you'll pass several ponds along the trail. Also, you might come across a few scenic high walls from an old coal-mining operation. The woods are mainly pine forest and white oak, and you're likely to see many spots where the beavers have redesigned the trees. You might want to stop by the old, historic coal-mining town of New Lexington, home of General J. MacGahan, a famous Civil War general.

General location: Off OH 345, 3.5 miles north of New Lexington.
Elevation change: There are some hills, but nothing dastardly.
Season: The summer and fall, when the ground is drier, are best. In June, there are several scheduled events for horse riders.
Services: Camping is available at Perry Trail Campground, but bring your own water. For bike service, go to The Wheel and Spoke Bike Shop in Zanesville.
Hazards: Be aware of horses, especially coming around blind turns. The horse tracks shouldn't be a problem since the trails are often groomed.
Rescue index: There are several roads in the area where you could flag down traffic. You'll also find a clear-cut where a buried gas pipeline runs. Follow the clear-cut to Possum Run Road, which will take you to OH 345. From there, it's less than a mile back to the campground.
Land status: Private property. The day fee is $2.50 to use the trails. If you camp here, trail use is included with the camping fee.

RIDE 15 *PERRY TRAIL CAMPGROUND*

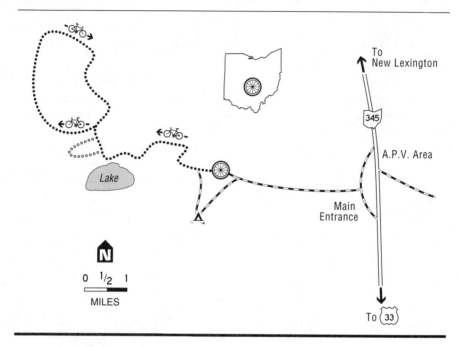

Maps: The USGS 7.5 minute quad map is New Lexington.

Finding the trail: From Interstate 70 and OH 13, take OH 13 south about 15 miles into New Lexington. Take a left in New Lexington at the traffic light onto OH 345. Take OH 345 north for 3.5 miles to the campground. The folks at the campground will direct you to the trailhead.

Sources of additional information:

> Perry Trail Campground
> 5200 State Route 345 NE
> New Lexington, OH 43764
> (614) 342-0601

> Wheel and Spoke Bike Shop
> 634 Main Street
> Zanesville, OH 43701
> (614) 453-3438

Notes on the trail: The trail is well marked. The markings will be on your left side going out and your right side coming back. The main loop is blazed in orange. Pink blazes will take you down the more difficult spurs and blue blazes will take you to the ponds (if you want to water your bike with the horses).

RIDE 16 *TOM HAYES FARM*

"This is training ground for West Virginia," says Tom Hayes, owner of the land on which this trail is found. I've never ridden in West Virginia, but I think I have an idea of what he means. Dan German, a local mountain bike racer, explains more simply: "It's really hard, one of the most difficult in the state." This I understand. In fact, I don't mind telling you that I took the worst spill I've ever had here at Tom Hayes Farm—but I enjoyed the ride anyway. This six-and-a-half-mile dirt single-track forms a loop with a few spurs departing from the main trail and joining it later. The elevation increases about 400 feet on this fast course, requiring strong technical ability and stamina to pedal up long and steep ravines, jump ditches (I can still feel my ribs ache), fly over moguls, and avoid rocks and ruts. You'll fight to keep your balance on sections where the trail is cut at an angle along the hillside. No wonder this place is a popular spot for local mountain bike races.

While the main loop is for those who know what they're doing, the spurs off the main loop are for those who know even more. For instance, in one spot on the main trail, you'll see a cutoff for the experts at the bottom of a steep hill. If you take that, you'll need to hike-and-bike in spots where the trail is only a foot wide and drops four feet straight down. Then you'll ride up a creek bed of loose shale before hitting another hike-and-bike section up a steep ravine. Of course, if you have wings, you won't need to do this part.

The area has historical significance as well. From an overlook on the trail, you'll be able to see the kiln fire walls of an old coal-burning power plant that supplied all the power from Columbus to Kentucky, as well as a little of Indiana and West Virginia. In fact, the plant is listed in the German archives as a bombing site in World War II. There are also a few Indian mounds toward the end of the trail. In the fall when the leaves are down, you can see the churches and buildings of the small town of Philo.

Bear tracks have been spotted out here, but not the bears. However, you are likely to spy coyote, deer, grouse, and pheasant among the buckeye, hickory, white oak, blue gum, elm, ash, and maple. Finally, legend has it that a famous East Coast painter originally owned this area years ago and used it for his own personal brothel. I can't verify this, but I do know you'll need all your energy for this trail.

General location: Off OH 60, 10.5 miles from Interstate 70 in Zanesville.

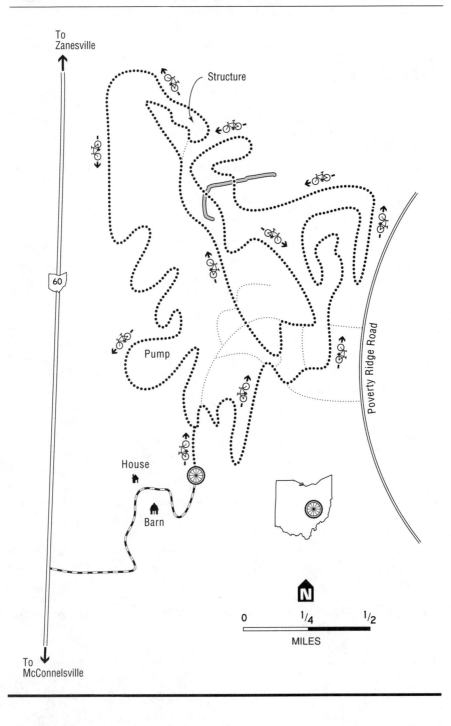

To Zanesville

Structure

60

Pump

House

Barn

Poverty Ridge Road

To McConnelsville

N

0   1/4   1/2

MILES

Dan won't have time to relax after fighting this uphill climb. On the other side, the fast downhill will throw a series of ditches at him.

Elevation change: The elevation begins around 830 feet and gains between 350 and 400 feet.

Season: The fall is a nice time to ride; the weather is cooler and the leaves are starting to turn. When the leaves are down, you'll get a better view of the towns of Philo and Duncan Falls.

Services: Bring your own water. All services can be found in Zanesville. For bike service, check out The Wheel and Spoke Bike Shop.

Hazards: The numerous rocks, ruts, ditches, and moguls will definitely challenge your technical skills.

Rescue index: Make your way to OH 60 and flag someone down. The town of Duncan Falls is only a mile away.

Land status: Private property. Before you ride, please check with The Wheel and Spoke Bike Shop about current availability. You ride at your own risk!

Maps: Since the trail is recent and likely to vary as the local riders work on it, you're best bet is to contact The Wheel and Spoke Bike Shop. The USGS 7.5 minute quad for this area is Philo.

Finding the trail: From the intersection of I-70 and OH 60 in Zanesville, take OH 60 south for 9.5 miles. After you pass the turn-off for Blue Rock State Park just outside Duncan Falls, go another .8 mile and look for a rock outcropping on your left. Turn left into the gravel entrance by this rock outcropping, and eventually you'll come to a farmhouse and a barn. Curve to the right and head toward the barn. Go past it to where the road turns into dirt double-track. (You're following the tree line.) You can park along the trees or in the field area. You'll see a break through the trees at the back of the clearing where you can begin the ride.

Sources of additional information:

The Wheel and Spoke Bike Shop
634 Main Street
Zanesville, OH 43701
(614) 453-3438

Notes on the trail: The trail is marked, but if you get turned around, follow the arrows backwards. They will return you to your car.

RIDE 17 *OHIO POWER RECREATION LAND*

If you want to take a family vacation where you can camp, fish, and hike, and you also want to take the family out for some easy mountain biking, Ohio Power ReCreation Land is the place for you. This area, covering 30,000 acres, is a reforested coal strip mine area. There are over 350 lakes and ponds stocked with fish, so bring along a fishing pole. The ride I describe below is a mix of gravel and paved roads, so your serious mountain biker won't find it too challenging. However, this 25-mile ride, including the distance along the main loop and the out-and-back spurs, does maximize the gravel roads, most of which head in and out of the various camping areas. This is ideal for the family that owns mountain bikes and has been searching for an easy place to ride them.

You won't need much in the way of technical skills, just enough to dodge a little traffic on the major roads, which, unfortunately, you'll probably have to spend some time on. You will need a modest amount of energy. While the gravel roads around the parksite areas are flat, OH 78 and OH 83, the primary paved roads, contain rolling hills, so be prepared.

The scenery in this area is worth the trip. You'll pass along the border of the restricted strip mine area, which offers an intriguing view of the mining operations. In addition, you'll ride by several scenic views of tree-covered valleys. In some areas, you'll get the chance to look back 300 million years at steep rock cliffs exposing layers of clay, sandstone, shale, limestone and slate. Down parksite D, Sawmill Road, you'll even find a small covered bridge. Among the animals you might see here are large mouth bass, channel catfish, northern pike, and chain pickerels. If you don't bring your fishing pole and an Ohio fishing license, then you'll have to be content with the blue heron, woodchucks, beaver, fox, and deer. In short, come for the camping and stay for the cycling.

RIDE 17 *OHIO POWER RECREATION LAND*

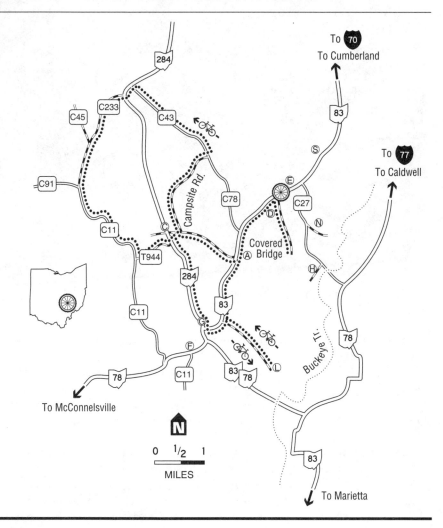

General location: In Morgan, Muskingum, and Noble counties, 22 miles southeast of Zanesville and 28 miles northwest of Marietta.

Elevation change: The elevation change is negligible on most of the gravel roads, and the paved roads contain gently rolling hills.

Season: Ride here during any season, but the alders, sycamores, silver maples, poplars, and ash will look fantastic in the fall.

Services: You can camp at the parksites, which have water and sanitary facilities,

One of Ohio's small covered bridges can be found on a quiet gravel road at ReCreation Land.

but no electricity. Reinersville has a few food shops. All services can be found in Zanesville.

Hazards: You should pay attention to vehicular traffic, especially on OH 83 and OH 78.

Rescue index: There's a phone at parksite E. Otherwise, traffic can be flagged down on any of the major roads. You'll frequently find campers down the parksite roads.

Land status: The land is owned by Ohio Power Company and managed, in part, by the Ohio Department of Natural Resources. You'll need to get a free permit from Ohio DNR or any Ohio Power Company office if you plan on camping, hunting, or fishing in the area. Write them at the address below.

Maps: You can get a map of the ReCreation Land area showing the boundaries and the restricted areas for Ohio DNR by writing the Department of Natural Resources at the address below. The USGS 7.5 minute quad for this area is mostly Reinersville, with a little of the area in the Cumberland, Ruraldale, and McConnelsville quad maps.

Finding the trail: From Interstate 77: Take Exit 25, OH 78, west for 10 miles. Turn left on Morgan County Road 27 (3 miles before the junction of OH 83). Take CR 27 for 3.5 miles and turn left onto OH 83. Almost immediately you'll see parksite E, Windy Hill, on your right.

From Zanesville: From I-70, take OH 146 east for 21 miles to OH 83. Take OH 83 south 8 miles to parksite E.

Sources of additional information:

> Department of Natural Resources
> Fountain Square
> Building B
> Columbus, OH 43224-1327
> (614) 265-6659

> Ohio Power Company
> P.O. Box 328
> McConnelsville, OH 43756

Notes on the trail: The parksites and roads are marked. You can begin your ride from parksite E. Turn right out of the parking area and take OH 83 for a half mile to Sawmill Road, parksite D. Make sure to check out the covered bridge at the end of this 1-mile each way spur. Come back up Sawmill Road and turn left onto OH 83 again. Take OH 83 for 1.5 miles to parksite A, Hook Lake. Across from parksite A, on the other side of OH 893, there's a gravel road which you should take for about 1 mile. You'll find this stretch to be rather scenic, passing tree-covered valleys and rock outcroppings. When you get to Camp Site Road, turn right and travel along a cattailed wetland area for approximately 2 miles. When you reach Muskingum County Road 43 at the T intersection, turn left. You're now traveling along the border of the restricted area, which affords a view of the strip mine operation. Take CR 43 for 2.5 miles and turn left on OH 284. Go for a few yards and then turn right on Muskingum County Road 233 (also called Young Hickory). You're now skirting the border of the ReCreation Land area. The scenery changes here—you'll notice trees on your left and pleasant farmlands in the distance to your right. As you pass into Morgan County, CR 233 changes to C 11. When this road dead-ends in 2 miles, take a jog to the left. C 11 will take you to Bristol Township Road 944 (also called Bristol Church Road) 2.5 miles later. Turn left on TR 944 and go 1 mile to OH 284. Go right on OH 284 for 2 miles to OH 83. When you get to OH 83, turn left and take that a half mile to Horse Run, the road for parksite L. Go down the spur for parksite L, a meadow area with abundant wildflowers, before heading back out to OH 83. Turn right on OH 83 and take that 4 miles back to parksite E, where you parked your vehicle.

This is just one recommended route for Ohio Power ReCreation Land. Feel free to shorten it if you like or explore some of the other parksites not included here, such as parksite N. The area is picturesque. Don't let the fact that you'll need to ride on some paved roads detour you.

The Buckeye Trail also passes through ReCreation Land.

Wayne National Forest— Marietta Unit

Marietta, which follows along the banks of the Ohio River, is the oldest organized American settlement in the old Northwest Territory. It was founded in the summer of 1788. The Ohio River itself has been described as the "highway of settlement," "the avenue of frontier commerce," and "the dividing line between the North and the South." Call it what you will, the trails in this region are mastered only by the best riders.

The Marietta unit of Wayne National Forest has a different policy than the other two units regarding mountain bike usage. Here at Marietta, mountain biking is allowed on the hiking trails. If you are up for the challenge, head to this area, fraught with both covered and natural bridges, as well as caves and coves.

The Ohio state motto is "With God, all things are possible." On the trails described here, you'll need some divine guidance to get you through. Since these trails have been designed for hikers, they are generally narrower than those at the other two districts. Also, the numerous trail obstacles will prevent all but the best riders from gaining significant speed. These trails are not for the faint of heart. The switchbacks are formidable, the trail width often pernicious. In fact, several of these trails are so remote and isolated, if something were to happen to you, it could be days before you would be found.

Scares and caveats aside, the persistent mountain biker will enjoy the sheer physical exertion required to ride here. Also, the Appalachian foothills are most prominent in this area, creating quite a contrast to the flatter lands in the northern part of the state.

Every now and then, the United States Congress does something right. Take Public Law 96-199, for instance. This law authorized the development of the North Country National Scenic Trail (NCT), which passes through or near several of the rides in this area. In Ohio, parts of the NCT follow the Buckeye Trail. When completed, the NCT will cover approximately 3,200 miles, beginning near Lake Champlain in New York before making its way across that state, dipping across the northeast corner of Pennsylvania, and looping around Ohio. It leaves Ohio through the northeast corner and continues on through eastern Michigan, northern Wisconsin, and central Minnesota before finishing at the Missouri River in North Dakota. Needless to say, this rivals the Appalachian, Continental Divide, Trail of Tears, Pacific Crest, Iditarod, and Oregon trails in terms of distance. If you would like more information about the NCT, write to:

North Country National Scenic Trail
1709 Jackson Street
Omaha, NE 68102

RIDE 18 *LAMPING HOMESTEAD TRAIL*

Of the traditional hiking trails in the Marietta district, this one is perhaps the easiest. It will still require good bike handling skills, though, to navigate around rocks and travel up small hillsides. This mostly dirt single-track consists of two connecting loops; one is 3.2 miles long and the other is 1.8, for a total distance of 5 miles. The elevation doesn't change more than 200 feet, but you may have to portage over some deadfall. The 3.2-mile loop is a little steeper and longer than the 1.8-mile loop. You'll even find a few stream crossings to spice things up a bit on the smaller loop, but if it hasn't rained, the beds might be dry.

The trail begins in a section of pine that winds around the pond. Soon you'll be traveling along a creek and winding up the hill on the other side. This is the trail for the mountain biker with good bike handling skills who wants only a dash of technical challenge and more opportunities to ride a little easier. Even the coyote and her cub scampering off into the brush didn't seem too disturbed by my presence. The placidity of this ride is punctuated by purple, yellow, white, and orange wildflowers near the end of the trail.

General location: One and a half miles from the junction of OH 260 and OH 537, about 35 miles from Marietta.
Elevation change: The net gain is about 200 feet.
Season: The weather is drier in the fall, and the Indian summers have moderate temperatures. Ticks can be a problem in May.
Services: Primitive camping is available at Lamping Homestead, but you will need to bring your own water. All services are available in Marietta.
Hazards: You'll find some rock obstacles. Be careful, too, that you don't slip going up a hillside.
Rescue index: The nearest phone is at a gas station in Graysville on OH 26, about 3 miles north of the intersection of OH 26 and OH 537. There is light traffic on OH 537.
Land status: Wayne National Forest—Marietta Ranger District.
Maps: For fifty cents, the Marietta Ranger District will send you a map showing the topographical markings of the 5 trails in their district; write to the address below. The USGS 7.5 minute quad for this area is Graysville.
Finding the trail: From Marietta, take OH 26 approximately 30 miles north. When you get to OH 537, go west. (OH 537 is 10 miles from the junction of

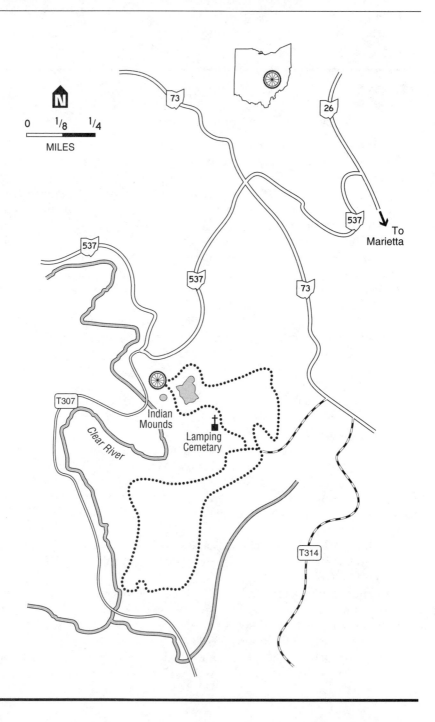

The wildflowers flanking the end of the Lamping Homestead Trail salute you as you finish the ride.

OH 26 and OH 260.) Take OH 537 for 1.7 miles and follow the signs from there.

Sources of additional information:

U.S. Forest Service
Route 1, Box 132
Marietta, OH 45750
(614) 373-9055

Notes on the trail: The trail begins through the pine trees by the picnic tables and is well marked by white diamonds. You won't miss the point where the 2 loops connect.

RIDE 19 *ARCHERS FORK TRAIL*

This nine-and-a-half-mile loop has much to offer those who like to cycle and explore. On the cycling side, the narrow dirt single-track passes through Irish Run and Jackson Run, affording you excellent views of the wooded hollows deep below. As you wind around the trail, you'll need bike handling skills to

RIDE 19 *ARCHERS FORK TRAIL*

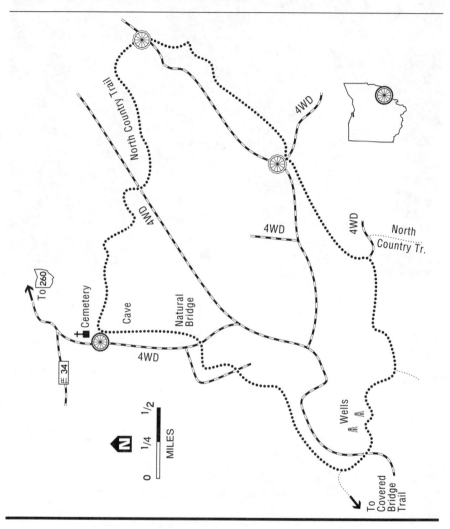

traverse deadfall, rocks, and similar obstacles. You'll see your share of rock outcroppings on a trail cut into the hillside. Most of this trail is rather steep. You'll even encounter a few stream crossings if the weather hasn't been too dry.

On the exploring side, you'll not only see (and smell) a few old oil and gas wells, but a couple of natural formations too. Consider exploring a cave at the bottom of a hollow. Signs will point the way. More unusual is the Irish Run Natural Bridge, which you'll find further up the trail. You can't ride across it,

Archers Fork Trail, on the way to the natural bridge.

but it's definitely worth getting off your bike to see. The arch is 51 feet long, 16 feet thick, and 39 feet to the rocky bottom below. Bring your camera on this ride.

General location: Wayne National Forest, about 4.5 miles from the junction of OH 26 and OH 260, roughly 30 miles northeast of Marietta.

Elevation change: You'll experience about 300 feet of elevation change.

Season: The weather in the fall is more moderate and the ground is drier than at other times of the year. In May, ticks are prevalent.

Services: Bring your own water. All services can be found in Marietta.

Hazards: Keep your eyes peeled for deadfall, rocks, and the usual hiking trail obstacles.

Rescue index: This trail is very remote, so travel with a partner. Even if you make your way to one of the intersecting roads, you may have to wait a while to flag down traffic.

Land status: Wayne National Forest—Marietta Ranger District.

Maps: For fifty cents, the Marietta Ranger District will send you a map showing the topographical markings of the 5 trails in the district. Write to the address below. The USGS 7.5 minute quad for this area is Rinard Mills.

Finding the trail: From OH 26 and OH 260, take OH 260 east. Go 3 miles to Ludlow Township Road 34 and turn right. TR 34 is easy to miss, so pay attention. Take TR 34 for 1.3 miles and you will come to an entrance labeled "North Country Trail." Turn in and park near the cemetery.

Sources of additional information:

U.S. Forest Service
Route 1, Box 132
Marietta, OH 45750
(614) 373-9055

Notes on the trail: Start the ride by traveling down an old dirt access road by the parking area. Soon you'll see a trail off to the left marked by the blue diamonds for the North Country Trail, which encompasses this section of Archers Fork. In a bit, you'll reach the intersection that takes you into the loop. Go to the right if you would like to visit the cave and the natural bridge on the first half of your loop.

The North Country Trail is marked in blue. The sections where the North Country Trail and Archers Fork run together are marked by blue and white diamonds. The sections that are strictly Archers Fork are marked by white diamonds.

If you break away from Archers Fork on the south end of the loop, you can follow the North Country Trail. Also, there is a connector trail which joins Archers Fork with the Covered Bridge Trail on the southeast end of the loop. The connector trail is marked by white blazes with a powder blue dot in the middle.

RIDE 20 *COVERED BRIDGE TRAIL*

Perhaps the most interesting attractions of this trail are not on the trail itself but at either end of it: covered bridges, one of which is still in use. Built over 100 years ago, these bridges over the Little Muskingum River take you back to a time when life was simpler. The trail itself is a five-mile, one-way (ten mile total), out-and-back, dirt single-track. Beginning with a couple of stream crossings, it makes its way out of the woods and into a field where the trail turns to grass flanked by beautiful wildflowers. Essentially, you're following a stream bed. Soon you'll enter the woods again, still following the creek. Enjoy the numerous stream crossings, but take care—some of them are rocky. After you cross over a pipeline, you'll start to climb. The last stretch of the ride puts you in a pine thicket. Then you travel downhill, eventually reaching the Hune Covered Bridge. This trail is among the easiest in the Marietta District, but good bike handling skills are still needed for the narrow trails, deadfall, and rocky stream crossings.

General location: Wayne National Forest, about 22 miles northeast of Marietta on OH 26.

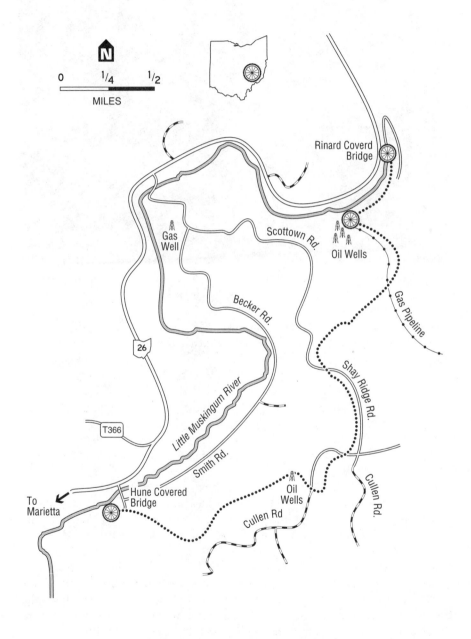

N

0   1/4   1/2

MILES

Rinard Coverd Bridge

Scottown Rd.

Gas Well

Oil Wells

Becker Rd.

Gas Pipeline

26

Little Muskingum River

Shay Ridge Rd.

T366

Smith Rd.

Cullen Rd.

To Marietta

Hune Covered Bridge

Oil Wells

Cullen Rd

Cullen Rd.

Between the covered bridges, this trail offers single-track riding and numerous stream crossings.

Elevation change: The overall gain is about 300 feet.

Season: Early spring and early fall are best, when fewer deerflies will annoy you and the weather is cooler. Avoid the ticks in May.

Services: Primitive camping is permitted at both trailheads, but bring your own water. All services are available in Marietta.

Hazards: Rocky creek crossings and deadfall may challenge you. Expect to portage your bike on occasion.

Rescue index: The nearest phone is at a general store in Wingett Run, 1.5 miles south of Haught Run Recreation Area on OH 26. Otherwise, traffic could be flagged down on OH 26.

Land status: Wayne National Forest—Marietta Ranger District.

Maps: For fifty cents, the Marietta Ranger District will send you a map showing the topographical markings of the 5 trails in the district. Write to the address below. The USGS 7.5 minute quads for this area are Rinard Mills and Dalzell.

Finding the trail: From the intersection of OH 7 and OH 26 in Marietta, you'll go 22.3 miles north and turn right on Washington County Road 406. After about a block, turn right into the Haught Run Recreation Area. You'll see the Rinard Covered Bridge right off OH 26 as a marker. Note: A few miles before the Haught Run Recreation Area, you'll pass the Hune Bridge trailhead access, but parking is better further up at Haught Run.

Sources of additional information:

U.S. Forest Service
Route 1, Box 132
Marietta, OH 45750
(614) 373-9055

Notes on the trail: As you pull into the camping area, follow the little loop around, and to the left of the toilet facility, you'll see the white diamonds marking the trail through the trees.

This trail has a connector trail to the Archers Fork Trail, which in turn links up to the North Country Trail. The connector trail is marked by white blazes with a powder blue dot in the center. To get to the connector trail, go up a hill to a road, where you'll see a sign directing you further up the road a little bit to the NCT connector on your left. To keep on the Covered Bridge Trail, you simply cross the road and ride straight through.

INDIANA

Northern Indiana

The slogan for a popular Indiana amusement park says, "There's more than corn in Indiana." That's true. There are also soybeans. The idea of mountain biking through an Indiana cornfield is not exactly a cyclist's image of daring adventure. After all, it's called mountain biking, not crop biking. (But if that ever catches on, remember, you heard it here first.) If you think mountain biking opportunities are few and far between in northern Indiana, well, you're right. There are two reasons for this. First, much of the area is relatively flat, agricultural land. The second reason is Indiana's Department of Natural Resources (DNR) mountain bike policy: mountain bikes are not allowed on DNR property. Perhaps someday we'll see an easing of this strict policy, but for now, it officially limits mountain bike opportunities in the state.

However, it is possible to find the occasional exception. Huntington Reservoir is one of them. While the land is managed by DNR, the property is owned by the Army Corps of Engineers, and they permit mountain biking here. Located outside of Huntington, known for its Romanesque Revival architecture and as the hometown of a former United States Vice President, the reservoir area has a trail that will test your technical skills—especially if you manage to ride there after the water level in the reservoir has dropped and the trail contains greater amounts of deadfall.

Not all potential mountain bike areas are state-run, as evidenced by France Park, one of the parks in Cass County. Park officials tell me that mountain biking is increasingly popular here and that riders often come up from the Indianapolis area. While most trails in this system are easily ridden, a few spots will test your ability.

If you're looking for perhaps the liveliest trail in northern Indiana, you have to move away from public land and look at private land. Outside Syracuse, local mountain bikers have taken matters in their own hands and created their own trail—a popular spot for races—at the Wellington Farm. If you want a definition for the term "switchback," come out here.

Thanks to Joe Fritsch, who helped supply information about the Wellington Farm, and to Keith Meyers, who assisted with Huntington Reservoir.

RIDE 21 *WELLINGTON FARM*

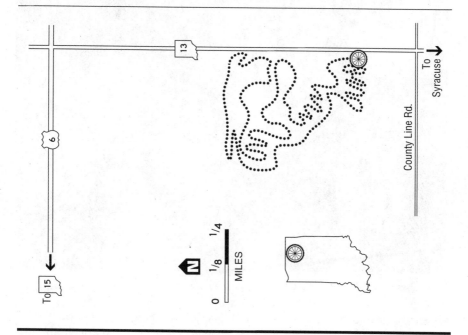

RIDE 21 *WELLINGTON FARM*

Switchback after switchback after switchback after switchback. . . . Don't be deceived by this short, four-mile loop, which is a dirt and grass, narrow single-track trail developed by local mountain bikers and used for area races. Your front wheel will be turning constantly from side to side on this one. You'll encounter switchbacks on uphills, switchbacks on downhills, and switchbacks just for the heck of it. "We wanted to make a course that was challenging to ride and challenging to finish," says Joe Fritsch, a local mountain bike racer. He adds, "This trail is much more like how mountain biking was four or five years ago when mountain biking was just starting. People would make it technical and challenging. Nowadays, so many courses are just wide open. Many mountain bike races follow dirt roads, so basically they're road races instead of mountain bike races. That's why we've gone to this style."

And challenging it is. On a dry day, you'll fight to maintain your balance. On a wet day—I shudder to think. You will enjoy the white-knuckle switchbacks,

Joe dashes to the next switchback, fighting to win the race.

especially the ones heading downhill. And no one will laugh at you if you decide to walk it around some of the intimidating ones. There are no major climbs, but that's no guarantee you won't be tested for endurance. I can think of one climb in particular that will cause you to struggle since you'll get no speed rounding a 180-degree turn.

The trail winding through the woods is narrow with a lot of climbs, descents, and gullies; look out for trees on those curves. When you get to the field, the trail is much wider, but it still winds its way through the grass. You'll have so much fun trying to negotiate this trail, you probably won't even notice the flora and fauna. If you do get off and portage, perhaps you'll see the many leopard frogs inhabiting this area. This ride is for the serious cyclist—in northern Indiana, of all places.

General location: Off IN 13, 1 mile south of US 6 in Syracuse.
Elevation change: The hills are short and the overall elevation change is nominal, but the constant up and down will tire you eventually.
Season: Late spring and early fall, when there isn't as much overgrowth, are the best.
Services: Bring your own water. Syracuse has food and lodging. Goshen has all services. For bike service, check out Hollinger Bicycles in Goshen.
Hazards: Look out for the trees on the narrower sections, especially the switchbacks. Obstacles on the trail are not as significant by comparison.

Rescue index: The area is not very large, so if you run into trouble, making your way back to IN 13 won't be difficult.

Land status: Private property. Before you ride, please check with Hollinger Bicycles about current availability. You ride at your own risk.

Maps: Since the trail is new and likely to vary as the local riders work on it, your best bet is to contact Hollinger Bicycles. The USGS 7.5 minute quad for this area is Milford.

Finding the trail: From IN 15 and US 6, go east on US 6 for 5 miles. Turn right on IN 13 and go one mile. You can park at the church at the corner of IN 13 and South County Line Road. To find the trailhead, ride back up IN 13 the way you came, and just past the guardrail, you'll see an opening through the trees for the trailhead on your left.

Sources of additional information:

Hollinger Bicycles
1410 South 10th Street
Goshen, IN 46526
(219) 534-2274

Notes on the trail: As you enter the trail, it's best to keep traveling forward. This is the direction that local riders traditionally go. You can ride the other direction, but if there are other people out there, you might run into someone. The trail is cut so that it often parallels another section of the trail. There are no intersections, however, so you won't make a wrong turn. Even though the trail is easy to follow, if you miss a turn, you may end up on a part of the trail on which you would have been in a few moments or, perhaps, were on earlier. (I once did that on a golf course fairway.) If you do get lost or if you come to the field section and choose to cut your ride short, you can always head east, and in no time you'll be on IN 13.

RIDE 22 *HUNTINGTON LAKE—KEKIONGA TRAIL*

Huntington Lake is used for flood control by the Army Corps of Engineers, and for this reason riding here can be a different experience every time you come. When the water levels are high, portions of this 11-mile loop dirt trail can be literally under water. After the water recedes, you won't know what to expect. Deadfall washed up by the floodwaters can present challenging obstacles to test your bike handling skills. Park workers clear the trails about three times a year, so there are times when it's easier to get through. Just before my first visit to Huntington, the disastrous Mississippi River flood of 1993 had peaked in the Midwest. The water was kept high at this reservoir to minimize water that

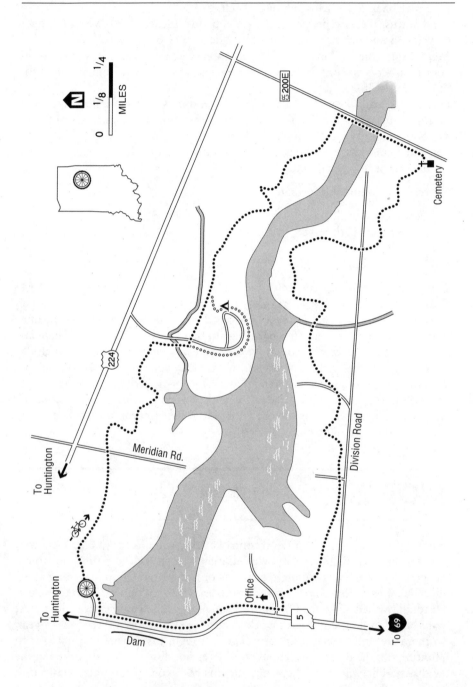

MILES

1/4
1/8
0

N

CE 200E

Cemetery

224

To
Huntington

Meridian Rd.

Division Road

To
Huntington

Office

Dam

5

To 69

would eventually make its way into the Mississippi River. I rode the trail just after the water had receded and I was impressed by the extraordinary number of branches deposited there.

Discounting the deadfall, the trail on the north side of the lake is straight and easy to follow, presenting just enough gullies to keep it interesting. The south side of the lake, though, is more complicated and technical since the single-track is narrower and rougher. There's a lot of heavy brush on this side and one tough creek crossing strewn with boulders. If you're looking for some technical riding, this is the side for you.

If you come in the winter, you might be lucky enough to experience what local mountain biker Nick Hancock refers to as "glacier riding." On occasion, the reservoir floods in the winter and then freezes. When the Army Corps of Engineers lets the water down, the "glacier" drops, causing the ice to crack and split. The ice covers the underbrush, and you can make your own trail through the trees. The area is home to deer, opossum, owls, and redheaded woodpeckers. Wildflowers like Queen Anne's lace, blue phlox, mayapple, and pasture rose add to the beauty of the area.

Oh, and how could I forget. Huntington is also the home of the Dan Quayle Museum. Need I say more?

General location: Off IN 5 in Huntington.
Elevation change: The short hills don't add significantly to the overall elevation change.
Season: The best riding is from mid-summer to late fall, when the area is not as muddy or flooded as other times of year. The trails could be completely under water after lengthy periods of rain.
Services: There's water by the Observation Mound. Camping is permitted at Huntington Lake. All services are available in Huntington. For bike service, check out Summit City Bicycles in Fort Wayne.
Hazards: Creek crossings and logs will cause you the most problems. Since the trail frequently changes with flooding, don't expect to find the same obstacles each time you ride.
Rescue index: You may find DNR staff by the beach entrance. Otherwise, you can flag down traffic on US 244 or Division Road.
Land status: The U.S. Army Corps of Engineers owns the land, but it's operated and maintained by the Indiana Department of Natural Resources. If you enter at the park entrance, the admission fee is $2.
Maps: You can get a map at the park entrance. The USGS 7.5 minute quad for this area is Majenica.
Finding the trail: From US 24 and IN 5, take IN 5 south until you see the sign for Huntington Dam Floor Control Reservoir—U.S. Army Corps of Engineers. Turn left into the entrance and swing to your right. Soon you'll see a wooden fence. You can park along the road there. You'll see a sign for the Scout Trail on your right.

Keith relaxes on a short grassy section after tackling the deadfall around the reservoir.

Sources of additional information:

Huntington Lake
517 North Warren Road
Huntington, IN 46750
(219) 468-2165

Summit City Bicycles
3615 North Clinton
Fort Wayne, IN 46805
(219) 484-0182

Notes on the trail: You'll begin the ride on the north side of the lake. At CR 200E, cross over to the southern side of the reservoir. You'll continue the trail by the cemetery. There's also a brown carsonite trail marker there. If you get lost on the south side, you can head south to Division Road, which will take you back to IN 5.

On the north side, you'll find a nice 2-mile section of dirt single-track near the campground. After you cross the water, you'll go another half mile, at which point you will drop into the paved road. Get on that and ride about a quarter mile. Turn left where you find another trail marker and you can enter the campground loop. Some of the jogs can get a little tricky, so pay attention.

RIDE 23 *FRANCE PARK*

This is a nice place for the recreational cyclist who's looking to get a flavor of what mountain biking is like on some easy trails. The various trails, labeled A through G, form a loop around and across the park area. Even though there are only four and a half miles of mostly dirt trails, you'll get plenty of variety: some bends on the trail, occasional root and rock obstacles, a few short hills, and views of the rock cliffs. After you try some of the easier trails, you can tackle Trail E, which is considerably more challenging. In fact, don't be surprised if you end up portaging your bike up a few steep, rocky areas. Because of the trail's short length, you may feel compelled to make a couple of laps around the park.

After you're finished riding, there's plenty more to do. Besides the fishing and swimming at France Park, you'll enjoy the water slide and miniature golf. The more adventurous can attempt scuba diving (bring your own gear) and rock climbing. Among the mulberry, dogwood, and pine, look for badgers, foxes, skunks, and raccoons. On second thought, don't look too hard for the skunks.

General location: On US 24, 4 miles west of Logansport.
Elevation change: You'll experience a few hills, but nothing to write home about. Trail E, while not offering a lot of elevation gain, is steep.
Season: I'd go in the summer. While the ice fishing and ice skating are nice complementary activities in the winter, I want that water slide!
Services: All services are available in Logansport. Camping and a store are also available at the park.
Hazards: You'll find a few roots and rocks. Take care while crossing the bridges, and remember, Trail E is rocky and steep.
Rescue index: The gatehouse is staffed and has a pay phone. Usually, you'll find other users on the trail and at the other recreational sites.
Land status: Cass County Park and Recreation Board. Day-use admission is $1 and well worth it.
Maps: You can get a map from the Cass County Park and Recreation Board at the address below. The USGS 7.5 minute quad for this area is Lucerne, with a small portion covered in Clymers.
Finding the trail: From the intersection of US 24 and US 35 west of Logansport, the park is 3 miles west on US 24. Once you're in the park, follow the main road around to the parking areas just west of the water slide.

Sources of additional information:

France Park
Route 6, Box 302
Logansport, IN 46947
(219) 753-2928

RIDE 23 *FRANCE PARK*

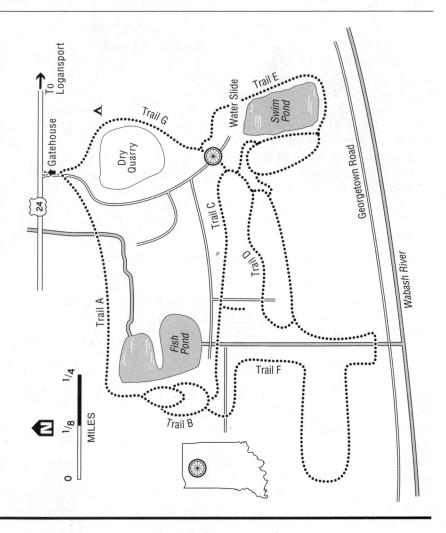

Notes on the trail: The trails are well marked, especially at intersections, and are easy to follow. Look for a yellow triangle trail marker or a silhouette of a hiker. You can begin your ride on Trail G at the east side of the parking area. This trail is mostly limestone gravel, but becomes dirt once you get up to Trail A. Trail F makes its way through the pines, and Trail E is the toughest, as it's narrow and steeper than the others.

With a water slide and miniature golf available at France Park, you just might want to leave your bike for some non-cycling fun!

Hoosier National Forest— Brownstown District and Bloomington

Indiana's motto is "The Crossroads of America." If you look at a road map, you will conclude that Indianapolis must be the crossroad point, since many major interstates meet there. However, I'd like to make the case that, as far as mountain biking is concerned, Bloomington takes the crossroads honors. For those interested in outdoor activities, this is the place to be. The Brownstown District of Hoosier National Forest is nearby, as is Yellowstone State Forest and the state's largest park, Brown County State Park. While the latter two do not permit mountain biking, they add to the beauty of this rugged area. There are many scenic drives in this region. In fact, along some roads near the forests and parks, expect to find heavy traffic in the fall as motorists ramble along, viewing the fall colors.

As far as mountain biking is concerned, it's some of the finest around. The Forest Service has been working with local bikers to help make mountain biking possible. While there are wilderness areas you need to avoid, the two rides described here, Nebo Ridge and Porter Hollow, offer hard-core mountain bikers challenges they didn't think they could find in Indiana. You will not be disappointed by the narrow single-track, old logging roads, and four-wheel-drive roads weaving in and out of the ridges of Hoosier National Forest.

Nor will you be disappointed by Gnaw Bone. While not as technically challenging as the Hoosier trails, this area has a flavor all its own, with its rustic cabins and dining hall and the wide, clean trails suitable for all riders. And if the Bloomington area seems like a mountain bike–friendly place, let Wapehani Mountain Bike Park serve as a testament. Although small in size, this city park is one of the few areas in this guide offically designated for mountain bike use. If that isn't progressive, what is?

Special thanks to Charlie McClary, who helped supply information for the rides in this area.

RIDE 24 *NEBO RIDGE*

Nebo Ridge in Hoosier National Forest is a great place to come for challenging single-track riding through dense woods. The main loop is 15 miles long, but there are over 60 miles of single-track, dirt roads, gravel roads, and four-wheel-drive roads. In fact, one stretch even follows an old pioneer wagon road. Some of the dirt roads are flat, but the uphill and downhill single-track is quite challenging. In certain sections, you'll even need to hike-and-bike. Rocks and ruts make for white-knuckled descents. No wonder The Flying Banditos, an informal group of mountain bike riders, come here to test their bike handling skills.

You'll ride along ridges, cross streams, and pass feeder ponds that make great camping spots. The vegetation in this mostly wooded area is among the most varied in the state. Most of the fauna hang out at nearby Brown County State Park, but you may find deer and wild turkey. The single-track is narrow, rocky, and rutted, but the sections on four-wheel-drive roads are a little easier to navigate. As one Flying Bandito member said of one of the best downhills around, "You can get in your big chain ring and just have a blast."

Nearby Nashville has many curio shops to visit. Nebo Ridge is also near Story, a small tourist town with a popular bed-and-breakfast well known for its good food. Of course, after you tackle the challenges of Nebo Ridge, my hunch is that you'll go for the bed part first.

General location: Outside Story, approximately 35 miles east of Bloomington.
Elevation change: The total elevation change is about 300 feet.
Season: The best time to ride is from June through early October. January through February is also good if the ground is frozen. In the spring, the trails can be quite wet, and in the fall, you run into hunting season; as one local rider puts it, "The hunters out here will shoot at wind."
Services: Bring your own water. Story has food and lodging. Bike service can be found in Columbus and Bloomington. Check out The Bicycle Garage in Bloomington. The shop also might be able to tell you when a group of local riders is going out and if the trails are open.
Hazards: Many of the larger rocks can be extremely slick because they're constantly wet. Watch for deadfall, rocks, and ruts, especially on descents.
Rescue index: This is a remote area, so don't ride alone. You're never more than 3 to 6 miles from a road, but it may be difficult to flag someone down. There are a few houses in the area.
Land status: Hoosier National Forest—Brownstown Ranger District.
Maps: The USGS 7.5 minute quads for Nebo Ridge are Story and Elkinsville.
Finding the trail: In Story, take Elkinsville Road south through town. The road will turn from pavement to gravel. Go left 2.5 miles from Story at the first road

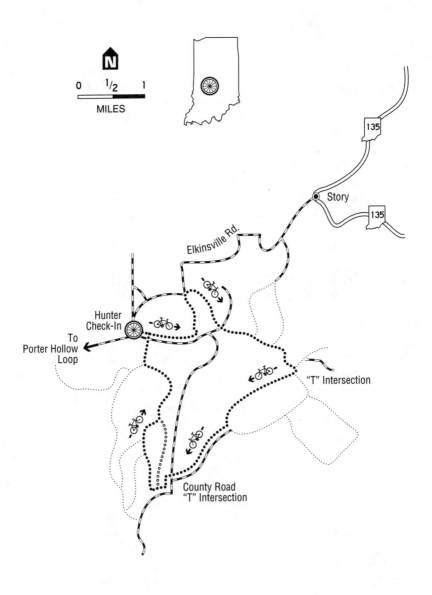

The old wagon road provides modern-day fun with its rocky descent.

turnoff. This road branches after a while, and you will take the left branch across a wooden bridge. Soon you'll come to a T, where you'll see a hunter check-in where you could park your vehicle.

Sources of additional information:

Brownstown District Ranger
608 West Commerce Street
Brownstown, IN 47220
(812) 358-2675

The Bicycle Garage
507 East Kirkwood
Bloomington, IN 47408
(812) 339-3457

Notes on the trail: From the T intersection where you parked your car, head east down the gravel road about a mile and take a left when you see a wide trail going up. Follow the trail up around the Wilkerson Hill area, and go left when the trail comes to a Y. (If you've bitten off more than you can chew, go right at this Y and you'll end up back at the gravel road. Go right at the gravel road and you'll be down near a creek). Go right immediately at the bottom of the hill crossing. Then go left at the top of the bank and follow the trail along the creek. For the pleasure rider, the trail winds through some gorgeous pines and old growth forest. For the hammerhead, the trail cuts some wicked single-track. The trail eventually crosses the creek on some slick, moss-covered bedrock and climbs an old wagon road. This part of the trail is steep, rocky, rutted, and fairly hazardous: be ready to get off and push. The trail flattens out on a ridge, so you can catch your breath and admire the dense woods. When the trail comes to a T, go right for one of the best "big ring" trails around. This section of trail rolls downhill, crossing a creek at the bottom. Once at the bottom, finding the trail can be difficult. Cross the creek and climb the bank on the other side, and the trail should appear. Due to its infrequent use, you may not see the trail immediately, but head right (west and downstream) down the valley. You will come to some fields. Look for a double-track trail here. It becomes more developed the further you ride, although you will have to ride down through the creek a couple of times. There are 3 or 4 fences and gates to cross. (Be sure to leave them as you found them.) The trail turns into a county road and Ts with another gravel county road; go left at the T. The gravel road skirts a hill and crosses a cement creek by a campsite. At this point you can take 2 trails. One is a wide old wagon trail directly behind you. For the other, go right into the campsite and follow the trail out the back. The trail goes left up a hill and up. There are several trails that spur off of this trail, but stay on the main one heading north. It will veer right and T with the wide wagon trail. Go left at this T and continue until you reach the top of Browning Hill where there is another wide wagon trail to the right. Take it. (If you'd like a good vista, continue straight along the ridge and you'll come upon a rock outcropping with a great view of Hoosier National Forest.) This downhill can be a white-knuckler, so use your brakes. The downhill ends at the original gravel road. Go left and you're almost back to your car.

Sound tricky? It can be. By the time this guide goes to press, the trail should be marked. This ride also connects up with the Porter Hollow Loop.

RIDE 25 *PORTER HOLLOW LOOP*

Located adjacent to the Nebo Ridge Loop, this 12-mile loop offers the same challenge: rocky, rutted single-track that will test your bike handling skills. On its south and east sides, the loop follows a fairly rutted, four-wheel-drive road. It travels through some lowland areas, so mud could be an issue. In fact, if you begin the ride from the boat ramp trailhead (not advised), you may even need to bring a snorkel. Find out the water levels on Monroe Lake before tackling this loop. You will have a few slippery creek crossings along with the usual obstacles you find in a dense forest—rocks, ruts, and deadfall. In the winter, this trail is especially nice because you'll be able to see far off into Porter Hollow.

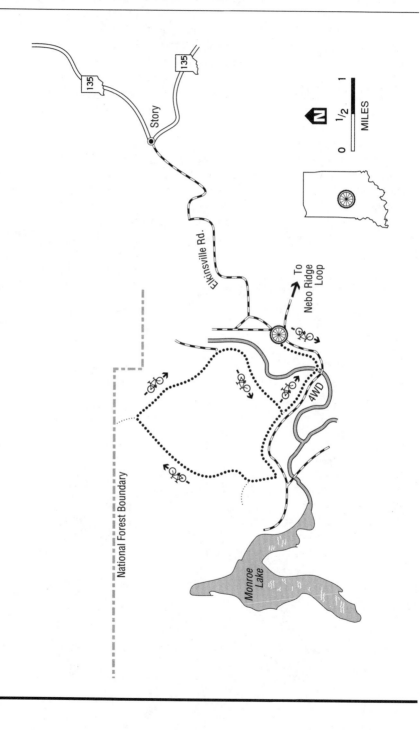

General location: Outside Story, approximately 35 miles east of Bloomington.
Elevation change: The elevation changes about 300 feet.
Season: The best time to ride is from June through early October, and from January through February. In the spring, the trails can be quite wet, if not impassable in parts. In the fall, you must contend with hunting season.
Services: Bring your own water. Story has food and lodging. Bike service can be found in Columbus and Bloomington. Check out The Bicycle Garage in Bloomington. The shop also might be able to tell you when a group of local riders is going out and if the trails are open.
Hazards: Slick stream crossings, rocks, and ruts will make your way challenging. Coming downhill into the lowlands can be quite muddy and tricky.
Rescue index: This is a remote area, so ride with a partner. While you're close to minor roads, they are not well traveled. There are a few houses in the area.
Land status: Hoosier National Forest—Brownstown Ranger District.
Maps: The USGS 7.5 minute quad for Porter Hollow is Elkinsville.
Finding the trail: From Story, take Elkinsville Road south. The road will turn from paved to gravel, and 2.5 miles from Story, you'll see the first road turnoff. Go left and eventually take the left branch across a wooden bridge. Soon you'll come to a T by a hunter check-in, where you can park your vehicle.

Sources of additional information:

Brownstown Ranger District
608 West Commerce Street
Brownstown, IN 47220
(812) 358-2675

The Bicycle Garage
507 East Kirkwood
Bloomington, IN 47408
(812) 339-3457

Notes on the trail: From the parking area by the hunter check-in, take the gravel road to the right. (To the left is the entrance to the Nebo Ridge Loop.) Carry your bike over the bridge—you'll see why when you get there. After you cross, there appear to be 2 trails. Take the one heading to your left. Follow this a little and take the first wide trail going off to your right. This is a wide four-wheel-drive road. You'll follow this up over a hill and then stay in the valley for a while, skirting along the edge of the hill. The four-wheel-drive road Ts at the gravel road. Go left. The gravel road ends at a campsite/trailhead, where you'll take the trailhead north and up. This section of trail is steep at first, but then flattens out to a more gradual ascent. As you ride, you'll notice several trails spurring off to the left. Make a mental note of these because you will come back to the last one. Eventually, you'll come to a big metal gate signifying the state forest boundary (off limits!). Now turn around, ride back down the trail, and take the first trail to the right. (Remember your mental note?) This trail is a

Four-wheel-drive roads on the Porter Hollow Loop will give you a chance to appreciate the scenery.

long, fun descent. Due to infrequent use, there will be a fair amount of deadfall across the trail. At the bottom, the trail turns into a grassy double-track. Soon the trail comes to the wide four-wheel-drive road that you came in on. Turn left and head back to the bridge and your vehicle. If you go right, you'll head toward the boat ramp trailhead.

This trail connects with Nebo Ridge.

RIDE 26 *GNAW BONE CAMP*

I knew I would love Gnaw Bone from the moment I entered the camp and was greeted by a host of golden retrievers. If you're looking for that self-contained area of mountain bike challenges and charming services, this is by far one of the best in the state. There are about 20 miles of well-designed and spread-out interconnecting trails through the woods. The trails are a mixture of single-track and old logging roads. Most of the trails aren't too technical; you won't find any obstacles to jump. The owners keep the trails clean, which makes them fun for people of all abilities to ride. You'll need stamina and endurance more than anything else.

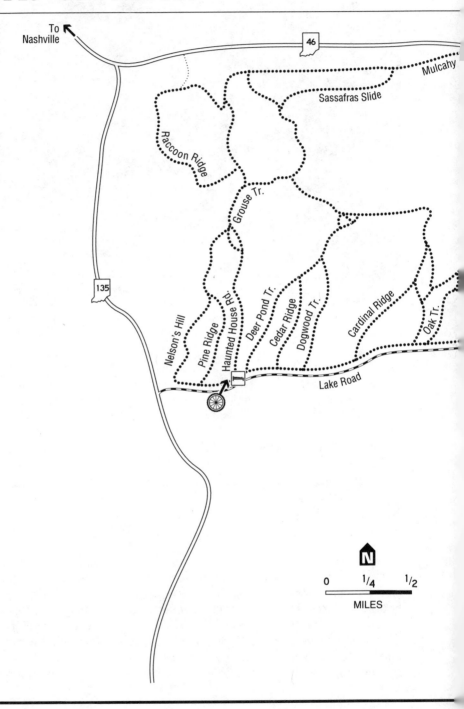

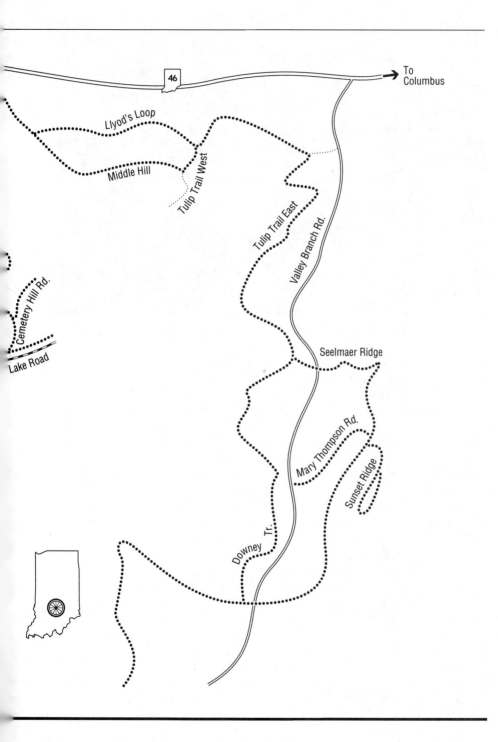

To
Columbus

46

Llyod's Loop

Middle Hill

Tulip Trail West

Tulip Trail East

Valley Branch Rd.

Cemetery Hill Rd.

Lake Road

Seelmaer Ridge

Mary Thompson Rd.

Sunset Ridge

Downey Tr.

Return to the past at Gnaw Bone Camp.

You'll encounter a few scenic vistas and several stream crossings. The stretch by Lake Road is flat and easy, as is the stretch called Mulcahy. One section near the Grouse Trail is affectionately known by local riders as "Return of the Jedi" because, just like Luke Skywalker in the namesake movie, you dodge pine trees on a narrow trail. Some of the trails follow ridges where you'll find streams at the bottom. In short, the riding here is good for experts and novices alike: The experts can push it for a good workout and tackle the few technical spots, and the novices can travel at a relaxing pace, sticking to less exhausting sections.

You would be remiss, though, if you came to Gnaw Bone only to ride. You will want to take a vacation here. When you pull in, you'll notice immediately that the place has the feel of the Old West. There are several cabins, a big dining hall, and a lodge with a fireplace, all built with a rustic feel. You can rent a cabin or stay at the hotel. You'll even find a museum containing natural wonders like animal skeletons, rocks, snake skins, and hornet nests. When you're done riding and checking out the museum, head down to the pond and play on the swing. Bring the spouse, kids, and whoever else knows how to have a good time. Gnaw Bone will supply the dogs.

General location: Twenty-two miles east of Bloomington on IN 135.
Elevation change: The overall gain is around 350 feet.
Season: You'll be able to ride here whenever the camp is open. There are 4 weeks in the summer when Gnaw Bone is rented out as a girls camp. The area

The trails at Gnaw Bone are suitable for all riders.

might also be unavailable if other groups rent it. The trails are used by cross-country skiers when there's snow on the ground. Bikes are not allowed on the trails when they are wet. Check first at the address below before coming.

Services: Lodging is available at Gnaw Bone. All services are available in Bloomington or Columbus. For bike service, check out The Bicycle Garage in Bloomington.

Hazards: You won't find many hazards. A few trails have rugged and rocky downhill sections, but you'll be able to see them coming.

Rescue index: If you need assistance, make your way back to the main lodge area.

Land status: Private property. The day-use fee is $2.50, but it's your loss if you only come out for a day. Also, you ride at your own risk.

Maps: The main lodge area has a map showing the different trails on the property. The USGS 7.5 minute quad is Nashville.

Finding the trail: In Nashville, take IN 135 south for 2 miles. You'll see the sign for Gnaw Bone Camp for Boys and Girls on your left.

Sources of additional information:

Gnaw Bone Camp
RR 2, Box 91
Nashville, IN 47448-9698
(812) 988-4852

The Bicycle Garage
507 East Kirkwood
Bloomington, IN 47408
(812) 339-3457

Notes on the trail: You'll see where to begin the ride from the main lodge. The trails are marked with signs indicating which trail you're on. Make sure you stay off any trail that isn't on Gnaw Bone property.

RIDE 27 *WAPEHANI MOUNTAIN BIKE PARK*

Why include a mountain bike ride where the main trail is only a mile long? Advocacy. Trail access is a volatile issue in many areas, but Wapehani, located near an urban area, is one public site designed specifically for mountain bikes. And in all actuality, it's not a bad place to ride, especially for enthusiasts who don't have a lot of time to devote to long workouts. Even though the main trail is a mile long, there are alternate trails that tack on a couple more miles. You will need technical skills on this mostly dirt single-track as you tackle ruts, stumps, and rocks. You'll also climb some hills. The trails go through woods and fields, and the main trail circles Lake Wapehani.

Wapehani Mountain Bike Park is only two miles from downtown Bloomington and is close to the Indiana University campus, so after the Fighting Illini beat the Hoosiers (sorry, Indiana fans), this is a great place to come to burn off the hot dogs. Charlie McClary, a local mountain bike advocate, sums up Wapehani best when he says, "It's small and compact, but it has everything."

General location: In Bloomington.

Elevation change: The elevation change is about 150 feet, and you will need to climb a few hills.

Season: It's open all year, but it gets crowded when the weather is nice.

Services: All services are available in Bloomington. For bike service, check out The Bicycle Garage.

Hazards: Your major concern will be the other bikes using the park. Wapehani is also open to joggers and hikers.

Rescue index: From any point on the trail, you're never far from IN 37, a busy road.

Land status: Bloomington Parks and Recreation Office. You will need to wear a helmet and have a bike waiver on file at the Bloomington Parks and Recreation Office or any local bike shop. Refer to the addresses below.

Maps: Bloomington Parks and Recreation can send you a map of the area. The USGS 7.5 minute quad for this area is Bloomington.

RIDE 27 *WAPEHANI MOUNTAIN BIKE TRAIL*

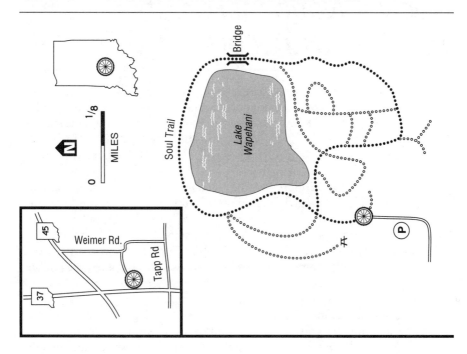

Finding the trail: From IN 48, take IN 37 south just over a mile and turn left at IN 45. Take IN 45 about a half mile to Weimer Road. Turn right and go another half mile to a sign pointing you into the park. You'll be able to spot the trailhead easily enough from the parking lot.

Sources of additional information:

> Bloomington Parks and Recreation Office
> 349 South Walnut
> Bloomington, IN 47401
> (812) 332-9668

> The Bicycle Garage
> 507 East Kirkwood
> Bloomington, IN 47408
> (812) 339-3457

Notes on the trail: Stay on the legal trails. If we bikers follow the rules, perhaps we'll see more mountain bike facilities available in the Midwest.

Hoosier National Forest—Tell City District and Selvin

Let's play word association. Indiana: corn. Kentucky: mountains. If your responses are similar to these, give yourself a failing grade. Consider this: If a mountain bike club from Kentucky comes to Indiana to ride, could the state be that flat? The members of the Kentucky Trailmen know better. From Louisville, Kentucky, club members frequently travel to the Tell City District to cash in on the mountain bike opportunities there.

Contrary to the flat farmland of the northern part of the state, southern Indiana is much more rugged. Here, you'll find many forests and limestone outcrops. The area is hilly—a region of dense forests and hidden valleys. It gives quite a different impression than the rest of the state.

As for mountain bike riding, the trails in the Tell City District of Hoosier National Forest can be quite isolated. "I love the wilderness of it—the remoteness," says Bruce Montana, a member of the Kentucky Trailmen. "You'll go out there and not see a lot of people. You're out there by yourself." He's right. When I visited the region, I was impressed by how secluded much of it was. And the riding will impress you too. You'll find caves, natural bridges, and other wonders as you ride some technically challenging trails. For the mountain biker who has the time, it's certainly worth the trip.

Slightly west of Hoosier National Forest is Yellowbanks, a private campground that has hosted several NORBA events. This is a popular mountain bike area offering challenging riding and excellent recreational activities. If you need a healthy mountain bike fix, the Tell City District of Hoosier National Forest and Yellowbanks would be the places to go.

Thanks to Bruce Montana and the Kentucky Trailmen, whose intimate knowledge of this area was tapped for the Tell City District rides.

RIDE 28 *HEMLOCK CLIFFS*

Of the five rides in the Tell City Ranger District, this one is the most scenic. This collection of old logging roads, jeep trails, single-track, and ATV trails provides for a rugged, roughly 12-mile, multiple-loop ride. The rutted roads are not maintained, but despite this are not too difficult technically; however, some are fairly rocky. You pass along sandstone cliffs, streams, pools, canyons, and even waterfalls from some of the cliff overhangs when the weather is wet enough. You'll also find a few natural bridges and a cave into which you can ride.

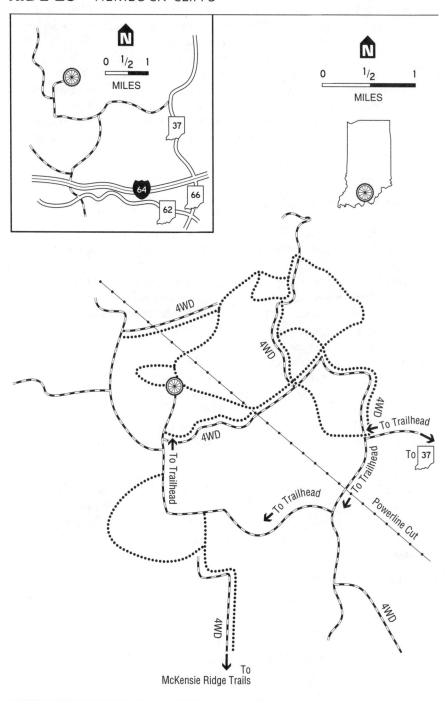

0 1/2 1
MILES

37

64

66

62

0 1/2 1
MILES

4WD

4WD

4WD

To Trailhead

To 37

4WD

To Trailhead

To Trailhead

To Trailhead

Powerline Cut

4WD

4WD

To
McKensie Ridge Trails

A good rider won't need a lot of stamina to get through the ride, but if you find yourself a little tired, consider getting off your bike to enjoy those natural formations. When you're rested, tackle some of the various creek crossings. Along with the geological treasures, you'll also enjoy the biological ones in this dense forest, including wildflowers and—what else—hemlock. You'll pass by some farm areas as well. My visit to this area was a costly one: the Indiana State Police ticketed me near West Lafayette for not driving slowly enough, and then my van broke down five miles from the trailhead. However, the remoteness and beauty of Hemlock Cliffs helped erase the hardships—until I had to open the checkbook back home. I trust Hemlock Cliffs will relieve you of your worries as well.

General location: Hoosier National Forest, 5 miles north of Interstate 64 on IN 37.

Elevation change: The total change is about 350 feet. Many of the hills are along the old road beds, some of which are quite rocky. Most are pretty good for challenging uphill climbing.

Season: Almost any time is good to ride here because the road beds are wide. Thus, you'll find fewer weeds and high grass to obstruct your way. Avoid the area during hunting season in the fall and turkey hunting season in April.

Services: Bring in your own water. For all services, head to either Evansville, Indiana, or Louisville, Kentucky.

Hazards: Be careful around the cliffs. You don't want to fall off.

Rescue index: There are a few farms in the area. Otherwise, it's fairly remote. In an emergency, the trails are accessible by four-wheel-drive.

Land status: Hoosier National Forest—Tell City Ranger District.

Maps: The USGS 7.5 minute quad for this area is Taswell.

Finding the trail: From I-64, take IN 37 north at Exit 86. Go 2.25 miles and look for a gravel, unmarked road. There is a sign for Hemlock Cliffs at the intersection, but you will have to look carefully from IN 37 because the sign is set back a little. Turn left on this gravel road. Go 2.5 miles and you'll come to a fork with a sign pointing to the trailhead. Take the right fork, and in another 1.5 miles, you'll see a sign pointing you toward a turnoff for Hemlock Cliffs. The trailhead parking is another half mile, and you'll see the trailhead from the parking area.

Sources of additional information:

Tell City Ranger District
248 15th Street
Tell City, IN 47586
(812) 547-7051

Hemlock Cliffs presents a variety of geological formations to explore.

Kentucky Trailmen
P.O. Box 5433
Louisville, KY 40255-0433

Notes on the trail: You can create multiple loops out here. Several of them connect with gravel roads. Take a map and a topo with you and explore. You won't be disappointed. Remember, it's fairly remote, so check your map often and don't ride alone.

From the south end of the trail, you can access McKensie Ridge.

RIDE 29 *McKENSIE RIDGE*

This out-and-back with a loop option near the end travels along an old dirt logging road and some single-track to create a seven-mile (fourteen mile total) ride. The roads are not maintained and thus are fairly rutted. Like Hemlock Cliffs, you'll need some technical skills to make your way down these service roads, but the difficulty is manageable. The greater challenge might be the gradual climb up the ridge. The single-track will have rocks, roots, and other

RIDE 29   *McKENSIE RIDGE*

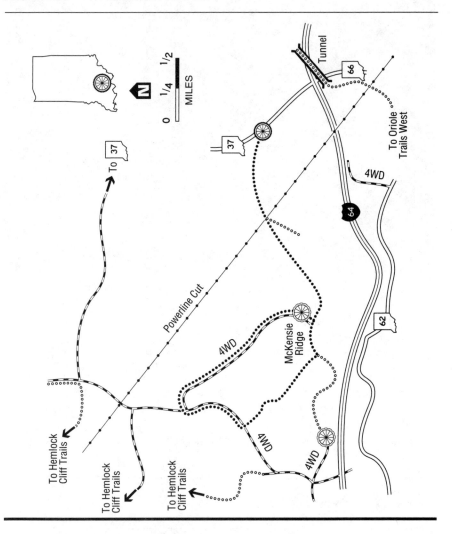

standard trail obstacles. While you won't find any stream crossings up on the ridge, you will find a pond built by the Forest Service to enhance the wildlife of the area.

The ride begins in a flat valley with ridges on either side. Eventually you make your way up 450 feet to the top of the ridge, where there was once a lookout tower. When you reach the top, stop at the pond, take out your Pocket Fisherman, and catch your lunch. South of the trailhead, you'll find a ten-foot wide, half-mile long tunnel under IN 37 by Interstate 64 that you can ride through.

General location: Hoosier National Forest, half a mile north of I-64 on IN 37.
Elevation change: The climb up the ridge is roughly 450 feet.
Season: Try McKensie Ridge year-round, although hunting seasons in the fall and in April are good times to stay away.
Services: Bring your own water. For all services, head to either Evansville, Indiana, or Louisville, Kentucky.
Hazards: No particular hazards on this trail aside from rutted and rocky stretches.
Rescue index: The area is remote, and you won't pass many houses. Most of the trail would be accessible by four-wheel-drive.
Land status: Hoosier National Forest—Tell City Ranger District.
Maps: The USGS 7.5 minute quads for this area are English, Branville, Beechwood, and Taswell.
Finding the trail: This trail can be tricky to find. From I-64, take Exit 86, IN 37, for a half mile north. Off to your left, you'll see a four-wheel-drive road. There is a small area—large enough for 2 or 3 cars—adjacent to that road where you can pull off. This road is the beginning of the ride.

Sources of additional information:

Tell City Ranger District
248 15th Street
Tell City, IN 47586
(812) 547-7051

Kentucky Trailmen
P.O. Box 5433
Louisville, KY 40255-0433

Notes on the trail: It wouldn't hurt to take a compass and a topo to gauge your progress. From the western corner of the trail you can access Hemlock Cliffs. Oriole Trails West can be accessed via the half-mile tunnel under the IN 37 exit.

RIDE 30 *ORIOLE TRAILS WEST*

There are over 20 miles of multiple-loop dirt trails in the west section of the Oriole Trails, one of the favorites of the Kentucky Trailmen. These unmaintained trails are comprised of old logging roads, ATV trails, and hunters' trails. More difficult than the other trails in the Tell City Ranger District, these sport

RIDE 30 *ORIOLE TRAILS WEST*

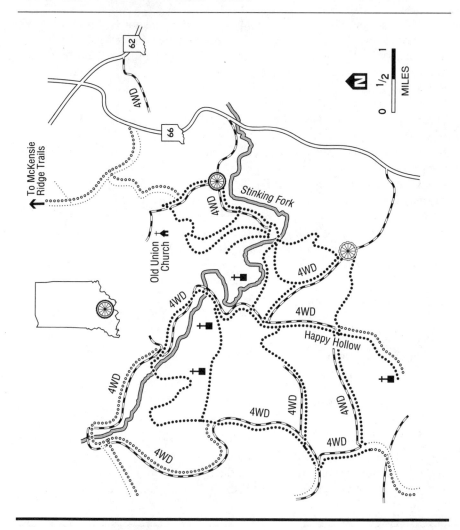

several steep climbs to test your endurance. There is over 300 feet of elevation change as you ride from ridge tops to valleys. Some of the downhills are steep and rutted, adding to the difficulty. A section of uphill on the Happy Hollow creekbed is especially jarring, and several water crossings add to the demands.

Oriole Trails West is a good place for the general outdoors person to come. On the ride, you'll get a scenic view of Stinking Creek as you travel next to the

Oriole Trails West is a prime example of the ruggedness in southern Indiana.

water. In addition, there are several wildlife ponds that could make campsites, especially in the Happy Hollow area. You'll enjoy the remoteness of this region.

General location: Hoosier National Forest, 2.5 miles south of Interstate 64 on IN 66.
Elevation change: There is roughly 300 feet of elevation change.
Season: You can ride any time, but be wary of hunters during the fall and spring hunting seasons.
Services: You'll need to bring your own water. For all services, head to either Evansville, Indiana, or Louisville, Kentucky.
Hazards: The steep and rutted downhills present the greatest hazards.
Rescue index: The area is remote. You'll find only a few houses. The roads are mostly accessible by four-wheel-drive, but there are gates across some entrances.
Land status: Hoosier National Forest—Tell City Ranger District.
Maps: The USGS 7.5 minute quads for this area are Beechwood and Branchville.
Finding the trail: From I-64, take IN 66, Exit 86, south and go 2.7 miles. On your right, you'll see a gravel road where you will turn. (It's just before the river by a sign for Sulphur Springs. If you've crossed the county line, you've gone too far.) In 0.6 miles, you'll see a little area where you can pull your vehicle off to

the side. It's not an official parking area, but you will see the trailhead across the road on your left.

Sources of additional information:

> Tell City Ranger District
> 248 15th Street
> Tell City, IN 47586
> (812) 547-7051

> Kentucky Trailmen
> P.O. Box 5433
> Louisville, KY 40255-0433

Notes on the trail: Because of the countless unmarked trail intersections, it is easy to get lost in this area. In addition to a "What, me worry?" attitude, bring along a compass and a topo, and plan to explore this region.

From the trailhead, you can access Oriole Trails East by riding 2.5 miles south on IN 66. From the northeast end of the trail, you can access McKensie Ridge via the half-mile tunnel under the IN-37 exit.

RIDE 31 *ORIOLE TRAILS EAST*

Only hard-core riders will be able to master Oriole Trails East; this is a truly rugged ride. While there are several dead-end spurs, the ten miles of trails basically form three loops. There is more single-track riding than on the other trails in the Tell City District, but you'll also find your share of old dirt logging roads, ATV trails, and pipeline cuts. In one section of the service road, the two-inch stone base makes for particularly bumpy riding.

This area will test your technical skills more than your stamina, not necessarily at the one water crossing, but via the many log obstacles. There are no unusual geological formations here, but the woods are scenic nonetheless. You'll discover a couple of wildlife ponds and pine groves.

General location: Hoosier National Forest, 5 miles south of Interstate 64 on IN 66.

Elevation change: There are no major hills. The overall elevation change is 300 feet.

Season: With the exception of the fall and spring hunting seasons, you can ride this trail year-round. You may find that the briars are quite overgrown in the summer.

Services: You'll need to bring your own water. For all services, head to either Evansville, Indiana, or Louisville, Kentucky.

RIDE 31 *ORIOLE TRAILS EAST*

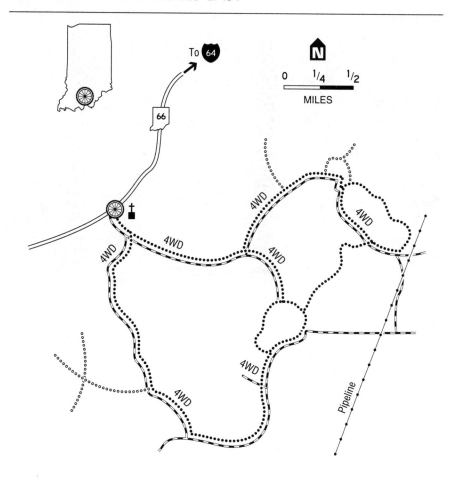

Hazards: As you would anywhere else, use caution crossing over logs.

Rescue index: This area is quite remote and you won't find any houses. The single-track makes four-wheel-drive accessibility difficult. Take heed: don't ride alone.

Land status: Hoosier National Forest—Tell City Ranger District.

Maps: The USGS 7.5 minute quad for Oriole Trails East is Beechwood.

Finding the trail: From I-66, take IN 66, Exit 86, south for 5 miles. On your right, you'll see a sign for the Oriole Pond parking area.

A rare grassy portion among the rugged single-track trails.

Sources of additional information:

Tell City Ranger District
248 15th Street
Tell City, IN 47586
(812) 547-7051

Kentucky Trailmen
P.O. Box 5433
Louisville, KY 40255-0433

Notes on the trail: From the parking lot, head north up IN 66 a few yards, and on your right you'll see Jeffries Cemetery. The trailhead heads off into the grass to the right of the cemetery.

Oriole Trails East is the most remote of the trails in the Tell City District, so you should not travel it alone. From the trailhead, you can ride 2.5 miles north up IN 66 to access the trailhead for Oriole Trials West.

RIDE 32 *MOGAN RIDGE*

There are over 30 miles of multiple loops you can make in the Mogan Ridge area of Hoosier National Forest. In addition to the loops, you'll find many dead-end spurs. Some of these spurs used to form loops, but since the trails are not maintained, they have since closed up. The trail network consists of old logging roads that make for a difficult, rugged ride, especially because the area is heavily used by horses. It's even tougher when the trails are soft and wet.

You'll find a deep creek crossing by Indian Fork. When the water is high, you will have to carry your bike across the water. You may need to get off the trail to find the high ground where you can cross. On the trail, you'll see a large over-hanging rock formation as well as numerous farm ponds. In the fall when the leaves are down, you can enjoy a scenic view of the Ohio River on the east end of the trail.

General location: Hoosier National Forest, 37 miles south of Interstate 64 on IN 37.

Elevation change: The grade can be fairly steep in sections, but the overall gain is only 300 feet.

Season: You will particularly want to avoid this area during the fall and spring hunting seasons. Spring and winter riding may be best since the deer ticks and chiggers are abundant in the summer.

Services: Bring your own water. For all services, head to either Evansville, Indiana, or Louisville, Kentucky.

Hazards: Because of the numerous deer in the area, the deer ticks and chiggers are especially bad in the summer. I heard of one rider who had to be taken to the hospital after a ride because he had been bitten so badly. Let me know if you go riding here in summer so I can buy stock in insect repellent manufacturing companies.

Rescue index: The area is isolated, and it may be difficult to get through quickly since many sections are blocked by gates.

Land status: Hoosier National Forest—Tell City Ranger District.

Maps: Derby is the USGS 7.5 minute quad for this area.

Finding the trail: From I-64, take Exit 79, IN 37, south for roughly 10 miles. Look for an unmarked road to the left by the logging mill (old IN 37). Turn left on that road at the sign for Mogan Ridge. (If you pass the road and reach IN 70, you've gone 1.5 miles too far.) Take the unmarked road approximately one-half mile. Look for the radio tower—you can park by its base.

RIDE 32 *MOGAN RIDGE*

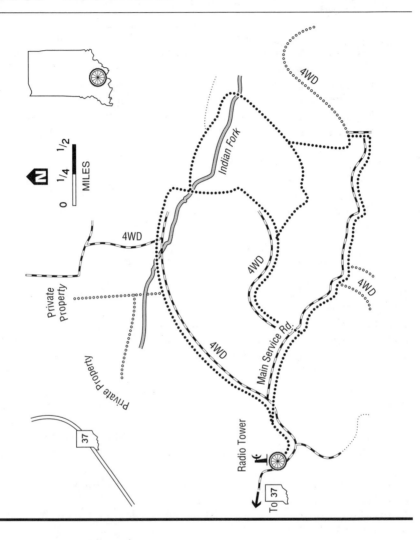

Sources of additional information:

Tell City Ranger District
248 15th Street
Tell City, IN 47586
(812) 547-7051

Kentucky Trailmen
P.O. Box 5433
Louisville, KY 40255-0433

Notes on the trail: The gravel access road by the radio tower is 5 miles long. To begin your ride, follow the gravel road and branch off at any of the logging or forest service roads and make the loop of your choice. The Mogan Ridge area is larger than this map indicates. Get yourself a detailed topo and delve into the southernmost of the 5 Tell City District trails.

RIDE 33 *YELLOWBANKS*

When I was researching this guide, one name kept coming up: Yellowbanks. Now I know why. A site for NORBA races, this is "the greatest trail—one of the best," according to expert racers. Beginning racers simply call it "tough." There are many climbs and descents on steep hills along this narrow dirt single-track. The trail depicted on the map shows the four-mile loop course used for the race, but there are many other trails on the property where you can ride all day. If you choose, you can also tack on about eight miles of gravel roads. The trail goes through heavy woods and contains several muddy creek crossings, some of which you'll be able to ride through, others maybe not.

The ride begins on the south side of the campground and passes a few lakes before heading into the woods. You'll find several sharp curves on the trail, passing through the trees. In fact, there's one rutted, muddy curve that may grab your front tire, and you could end up finishing the curve before your bike does. The trail passes near the edge of a coal mine, but you won't see much of it. You may, though, see deer, wild turkey, and coyote among the hardwood and pine forest. In short, you should find this an enjoyable, competitive ride in a rough, remote area.

Come for the riding, but stay for the extras. Those who ride here enjoy the facilities as much as the trail. There are many full-service campsites at Yellowbanks, and by the time this guide goes to press, there should be several rustic cabins available, too. When you're done riding, relax down at the beach. Hand-turned pottery from clay found right on the grounds is also made at Yellowbanks. Other nearby recreational opportunities include an amusement park and a visit to a small town called Santa Claus. How can you beat that?

General location: About 35 miles northeast of Evansville.
Elevation change: The elevation changes only about 40 feet, but you will find climbs both gradual and steep.

RIDE 33 *YELLOWBANKS*

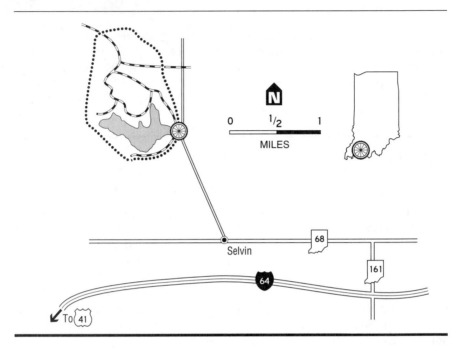

Season: It gets hot in the summer, so spring and fall are best. The dogwood trees bloom in the spring, and rumor has it that good mushroom hunting can be done then, too.

Services: Water and lodging are available at Yellowbanks. Bike service can be found in Evansville or Jasper.

Hazards: Deadfall isn't much of a problem. Stay alert on the turns, especially on the hills.

Rescue index: There's a phone in the campground. On the trail, you're never too far from the back of the campground.

Land status: Private property. The day-use fee is $1.50. You may need to sign in and out if you ride.

Maps: The USGS 7.5 minute quad for this area is Holland.

Finding the trail: Coming from the east: From Interstate 64 and IN 161, go north on IN 161 for .25 mile. You will come to a T. Go left. That will take you to Selvin in roughly a mile. In Selvin, turn north on the county blacktop (you'll see a sign for Yellowbanks). Follow the blacktop for three-fourths of a mile; the sign will direct you in.

Coming from the west: From I-64 and IN 61, go north on IN 61 about 1,000 feet to a caution light, and turn right onto old IN 68. Go 10 miles into Selvin and turn left on the county blacktop. Follow the signs from there.

Sources of additional information:

Yellowbanks
RR 2 Dale
Selvin, IN 47523
(812) 567-4703

Notes on the trail: The folks at the campground will direct you to the trailhead. The 4-mile course is marked for the races, but it may vary from the map as race officials change it around for each race.

ILLINOIS

NOTE: The 708 area code for phone numbers listed in rides 35, 36, and 40-42 will change to 630 on August 3, 1996.

Chicago Area: Out-and-Backs

At one time, most of Illinois was covered by expansive prairies, but that soon gave way to agricultural development. Then especially in the northeast corner of the state, in an area commonly known as Chicago and the Collar Counties, agriculture gave way to industry, commercial development, and housing. Prairies are almost a memory. However, you can still find vestiges of what this state was like in a bygone era. On several of the trails listed in this section, you'll be able to see restored prairies.

The trails described here all have one thing in common—they're out-and-backs. The Chicago area arguably has one of the highest concentrations of rails-to-trails conversions. Two are listed here—the Prairie Path and the Great Western Trail. In addition, you'll find one towpath trail, the I & M Canal, as well as one nature trail, the Des Plaines River Trail. All of these trails are easy to ride and suitable for all ages and abilities. Being an eclectic trail guide with a "something for everyone" approach, I've put these popular multi-purpose trails in one section for the benefit of those who want a relaxing ride. Hard-core mountain bikers should skip ahead.

Choosing which out-and-backs to include was a challenge. There are many fine trails in the area, but several are mostly paved and not included in this guide. The four trails in this section are located in areas surrounding Chicago. You should have something easy to ride in whichever direction you choose. If you want to ride the out-and-back trails east of Chicago, get yourself a jetski.

RIDE 34 DES PLAINES RIVER TRAIL SOUTH

Running parallel to the Des Plaines River for most of the route, this nine-mile one-way (eighteen mile total), out-and-back multi-purpose trail will give you an easy ride along its crushed gravel surface. You'll pass through woods, fields, and marshes with many views of the lazy Des Plaines River, as well as through MacArthur Woods Forest Preserve, a dedicated preserve which can only be accessed via the trail. Along the river look for beavers, turtles, and herons. Take the family and enjoy a relaxing day of riding. Feed the geese, go fishing, ice skate in the winter, barbecue at the picnic shelters, and let the kids go fishing, but above all, try this bike ride in the northern suburbs of Chicago.

General location: Off IL 22 in Lincolnshire.
Elevation change: Mostly flat.

RIDE 34   *DES PLAINES RIVER TRAIL SOUTH*

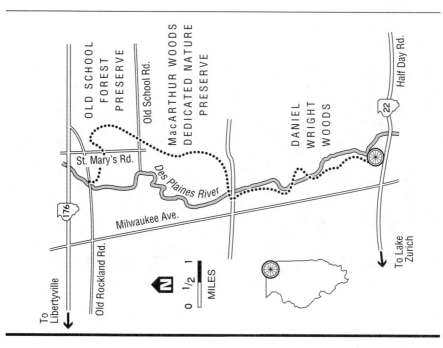

Season: Ride here all year long, but the fall colors along the river are especially pleasing.

Services: Water is available at the trailhead. All services are available in Deerfield.

Hazards: Since the trail is popular, look out for other bicyclists, hikers, or equestrians. Major road intersections have bridges and underpasses, so traffic is not a major concern.

Rescue index: The trail is well traveled and regularly patrolled by rangers and volunteers. There is a phone at the trailhead.

Land status: Lake County Forest Preserves.

Maps: You can get a trail map from the forest preserve district at the address below.

Finding the trail: From Interstate 94 and IL 22 (Half Day Road), go west on IL 22 for 2 miles to Milwaukee Avenue. Turn right on Milwaukee Avenue and go 1 mile to Half Day Preserve. Follow the directional signs to the trailhead.

   Contact Lake County Forest Preserve for additional places to pick up the trail.

Geese and cyclists, side by side.

Sources of additional information:

Lake County Forest Preserves
2000 North Milwaukee Avenue
Libertyville, IL 60048
(847) 367-6640

Notes on the trail: There is also a Des Plaines River Trail North, covering another 9-mile route. The north section has fewer woodlands and more open prairies and savannas. However, the 2 trails do not connect and are several miles apart. Eventually, the 2 sections will connect for a trail distance of 33 miles one-way.

RIDE 35 *ILLINOIS PRAIRIE PATH*

You can't write a guide that includes rails-to-trails conversions in Illinois and not mention the Illinois Prairie Path. This 55-mile one-way (110 mile total) out-and-back—following the route of the former Chicago, Aurora, and Elgin Railway—was the country's first rail-to-trail conversion and Illinois's first nationally designated trail. This trail was first established in 1966, with various

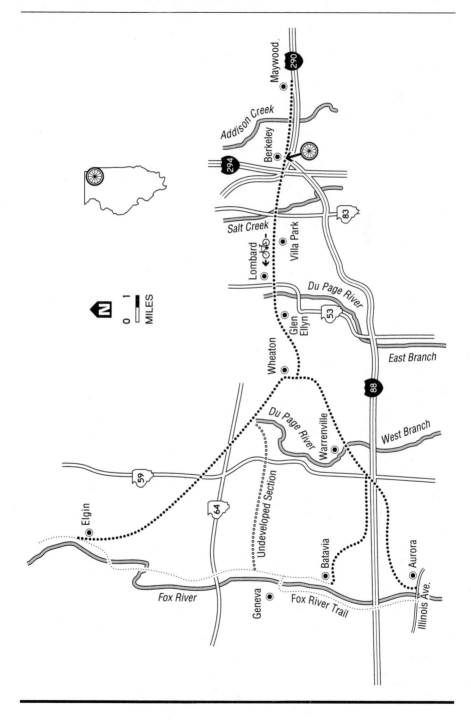

additions added throughout the years. Most of the path is limestone gravel; only a handful of spots contain asphalt to prevent erosion. The ride is easy and popular with bicyclists and hikers.

The ride begins in Maywood, but in the town of Wheaton it branches off in two directions. One branch heads northwest to Elgin and the other goes southwest to Aurora. A spur off the Aurora branch heads toward Batavia. Another spur, the Geneva spur, is not yet connected to the Elgin branch, but plans are underway to bring them together. As you ride the main branch out of Maywood, the trail is not very developed, but it improves the farther west you ride. Much of the main branch travels through suburban areas and, if nothing else, will give you a flavor of the communities in the western suburbs of Chicago. The right-of-way is mostly tree-lined, making for a pleasant ride. Also, there are frequent street crossings in this area. You'll pass through the downtown districts of Glen Ellyn and Wheaton. In Wheaton, be sure to admire the three spans of Volunteer Bridge, built by Prairie Path volunteers and welded by trade school students, at the Wheaton junction. If you take the southwest branch toward Aurora, the development lessens. You'll pass through some wooded areas and agricultural lands. On the Northwest branch, you'll pass a few more wooded areas, including the Pratt Wayne Woods where you'll find egrets, blue heron, and other wildlife.

General location: The easternmost edge of the trail is in Maywood. The Wheaton intersection point, near the middle, is often considered the starting point. The trail's spurs take you to Aurora, Batavia, Geneva, and Elgin.
Elevation change: Negligible.
Season: Ride the Illinois Prairie Path any time of year. In the autumn, the colors are beautiful. The trail is used most during the warmer summer months. It's less crowded on weekdays.
Services: Services can be found in many of the towns along the route, including Wheaton, Aurora, Batavia, Geneva, and Elgin.
Hazards: Look out for other trail users when the weather is nice and take caution at the numerous street crossings.
Rescue index: The area is well populated, so finding help should be no problem.
Land status: Various organizations manage the Illinois Prairie Path. In DuPage County, the Division of Transportation maintains the trails. In Kane County, the forest preserve district and the Fox Valley Park District are responsible. In Cook County, an association of the several municipalities as well as the Illinois Department of Conservation are responsible.
Maps: The Illinois Prairie Path, at the address below, can send you a map of the trail.
Finding the trail: People often pick up the trail at various points along the route. If you want to begin at the eastern end of the trail, you can pick it up in

The first rails-trails conversion, the Illinois Prairie Path tours the western suburbs of Chicago.

Berkley. From I-290 and St. Charles Road, take St. Charles Road east for a half mile to Taft Street. At Taft Street, turn right and go a half mile to the 4-way stop at Electric Avenue. Turn right at Electric Avenue and park in the lot a half block farther on your right, across the street from the fire station/police department/town hall. You'll see the trailhead easily enough on the west side of the parking lot. The trail actually begins a few miles to the east, but it is undeveloped at this portion and parking is more limited.

Contact the Illinois Prairie Path for additional places to pick up the trail.

Sources of additional information:

The Illinois Prairie Path
P.O. Box 1086
Wheaton, IL 60189
(708) 752-0120

Notes on the trail: The route is marked and easy to follow. You can find information about the trail at various kiosks along the way.

RIDE 36 *GREAT WESTERN TRAIL*

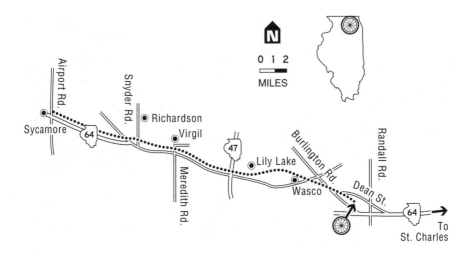

RIDE 36 *GREAT WESTERN TRAIL*

This 18-mile one-way (36 mile total) rail-to-trail conversion runs through rural areas on the outskirts of the Chicago suburbs. Ninety percent of the trail is limestone gravel and about ten percent is blacktop. You'll pass through agricultural, housing, commercial, and manufacturing areas. Even though you'll ride through these developed areas, this trail will give you a nice flavor of fields, marshes, and wetlands the farther west you go. In fact, you'll pass seven designated natural areas on the trail. You'll see several natural species of grass as well as abundant white-tailed deer, fox, and beaver. The trail runs from St. Charles in Kane County to Sycamore in DeKalb County. You'll pass through several old farming towns that you might want to explore: Wasco, Lily Lake, Virgil, and Richardson. Come see why Illinois is called The Prairie State.

General location: The ride begins on the western edge of St. Charles, west of Randall Road on Dean Street.

The Great Western Trail spotlights Illinois's Prairie State status.

Elevation change: Negligible.

Season: All seasons are good, but you might want to head out here in the spring to break cabin fever. Of course, the fall colors in the Midwest are noteworthy.

Services: There is water at the trailhead and at the various communities along the way. All services are available in St. Charles.

Hazards: Washouts after a heavy rain could cause problems. Also, look for mud patches at farm vehicle crossings.

Rescue index: You're usually not far from an intersection where you can flag down help. There are mile-marker posts along the route so you will know your location.

Land status: Kane County Forest Preserve District.

Maps: The Kane County Forest Preserve District (address below) can send you a map of the trail. The USGS 7.5 minute quads for the Great Western Trail are Geneva, Elburn, Maple Park, and Sycamore.

Finding the trail: From IL 59 and North Avenue (IL 64), go west 7 miles to Randall Road at the other side of St. Charles. Turn right on Randall Road and go north for a half mile. At the next traffic light, go west on Dean Street for another half mile. You'll see the entrance on the left side of the road.

Contact Kane County Forest Preserve District for additional places to pick up the trail.

Sources of additional information:

> Kane County Forest Preserve District
> 719 Batavia Avenue
> Geneva, IL 60134
> (708) 232-1242

Notes on the trail: The trailhead is apparent from the parking area, and the route is well marked and easy to follow.

RIDE 37 *ILLINOIS AND MICHIGAN CANAL STATE TRAIL*

Steeped in historical significance, this 55-mile one-way (110 mile total) former towpath makes for a beautiful, relaxing ride along the I & M Canal. The trail surface is base gravel with limestone. Riders of all ages will enjoy the serenity of this out-and-back trail, disturbed only occasionally by a "plop" as one of the countless turtles sunning on logs dives into the water or by the occasional boat and barge traffic from either the Des Plaines River or the Illinois River. Even though there is intermittent industry on the other side of the waterways, you'll be able to overlook that as you admire the variety of bird life along the canal. I've seen bluebirds, goldfinches, herons, kingfishers, woodpeckers, egrets, and scarlet tanagers. It's a bird watcher's paradise.

Aside from the turtles and birds, there are historical and natural sites to see. Where the Des Plaines, Kankakee, and Illinois Rivers meet, you'll see Dresden Nuclear Power Station across the way, the first nuclear power-generating station in the world. If you wish to go back in time, check out the various exhibits and relics from the era when the mule-boat teams used the canal to pull barges—old lock tender houses, locks, and aqueducts. Also, the state's biggest tree, an eastern cottonwood, can be seen near Morris. It was knocked down in a recent storm, but the remains are still there and you can get a good sense of what the tree was like standing. In fact, you can appreciate its size more now that it's down.

Near the canal in Utica is Starved Rock State Park, where you can climb to the top of Starved Rock for a breathtaking view of the Illinois River and the surrounding countryside. The town of Ottawa was the first site for the famous Lincoln-Douglas debates. A visitor's center in Utica and an information center in Gebhard Woods in Morris can provide much more of the history. Living so close to the I & M Canal, I may be biased, but when it comes to riding along old towpaths or abandoned railways, this trail is my personal favorite.

General location: The trail begins in Channahon and makes its way through Morris, Seneca, Marseilles, Ottawa, and Utica before finishing in LaSalle.

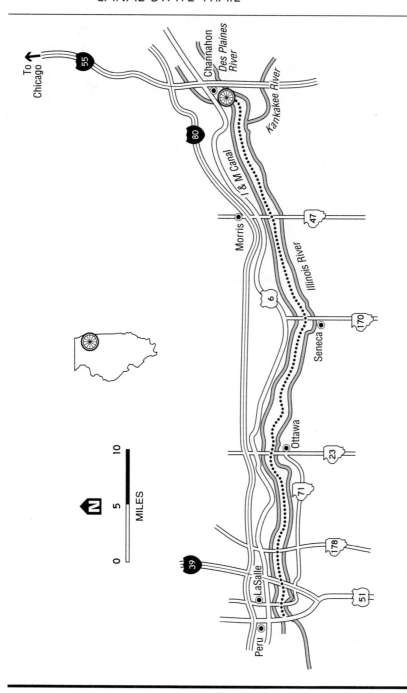

Ron and son, Craig, enjoy the historic towpath trail.

Elevation change: Negligible.

Season: Any time. I can't think of a time when I wouldn't want to ride here.

Services: Water is available at Channahon Access, AuxSable Access, McKinley Woods, and Buffalo Rock. Primitive camping is available at Channahon Access, AuxSable Access, McKinley Woods, and Gebhard Woods. Good bike shops can be found in Joliet and Morris. Seneca, Marseilles, and Ottawa all have fantastic mom-and-pop restaurants if you get tired and decide to rest in one of these authentic canal towns.

Hazards: Occasionally you'll pass other cyclists and hikers, but this trail is less crowded than others of its kind.

Rescue index: There are usually enough people around if you run into a problem. You can also find help in the various towns you pass along the way.

Land status: State trail.

Maps: You can get a map of the trail from the information center, visitor center, and ranger stations. The Heritage Corridor also has trail information; write to the address below. The USGS 7.5 minute quads for this trail are Channahon, Minooka, Coal City, Morris, Seneca, Marseilles, and Ottawa.

Finding the trail: Take Interstate 55 to Exit 248, US 6, which is 2 miles south of I-80. Go west on US 6 into Channahon, and 4.5 miles from I-55 (on US 6), you'll see a sign for the I & M Canal on Canal Street. Turn left and go down to the second stop sign. Turn right on Bridge Street. In another block, after you cross the first bridge, turn left into the parking area. If you cross the second bridge, you've gone too far. You'll see the starting point at the other end of the parking area.

There are other access points to the trail. Contact the Heritage Corridor Visitors Bureau for additional sites.

Sources of additional information:

Illinois and Michigan Canal State Trail
P.O. Box 272
Morris, IL 60450
(815) 942-0796

Heritage Corridor Visitors Bureau
81 North Chicago Street
Joliet, IL 60431
(815) 727-2323

Notes on the trail: The trailhead described above is a good place to begin your ride. The services at Channahon Access are on the other side of Bridge Street, down the trail about a quarter mile.

Chicago Area: Forest Preserves and Parks

Chicago is the third largest metropolitan area in the United States, and, as you may imagine, is not perceived as a mountain biking mecca. While there are a few nice paved bicycle paths in the city of Chicago, there isn't much in the way of unpaved trails. However, you don't have to get too far out of the city to find areas where you can do some serious riding, even though several of the rides listed in this section are surrounded by fairly well-populated areas.

Urban sprawl has created an interesting situation in the Chicago area. Cook County, where Chicago is located, and the surrounding collar counties all have county forest preserve districts. Scattered throughout this urban and suburban area, you'll find little pockets of wilderness where people in the city flock on weekends. Unlike expansive national forests, it's difficult to get seriously lost in a forest preserve. However, that doesn't mean you can't find dense woodlands. In fact, many of the forest preserves and parks here offer a variety of terrain, including woods, fields, prairies, and marshes.

As far as mountain biking goes, some of these preserves offer easy riding while others make up in technical demands what they lack in elevation. But don't be fooled. Areas like Swallow Cliffs and Deer Grove can have elevation changes ranging around 100 feet. It's not Colorado, but in an area where people think the tallest thing around is the Sears Tower, they're often surprised at what they find here. Some of these trails, like the Regional Trail, and the trails in Waterfall Glen and Moraine Hills State Park have neither technical challenges nor serious elevation changes, but they do provide a nice option if you are interested in the course prerequisite for Mountain Biking 101.

The trail descriptions that follow were written with the help of several people. Thanks to Bart Dahlstrom for providing information about Deer Grove, Duane Anderson and Mike Palazzetti for the Regional Trail and Elsen's Hill, Andy Pilska for Swallow Cliffs and Maple Lake, and Mark Karner for Hammel Woods.

RIDE 38 MORAINE HILLS STATE PARK

Moraine Hills State Park is a good place to ride if you're looking for a non-technical trail but still want a workout. The first time I visited here, I saw a couple on a mountain bike tandem pulling a trailer. "Easy ride?" I asked. "I'm sweating,"

RIDE 38 *MORAINE HILLS STATE PARK*

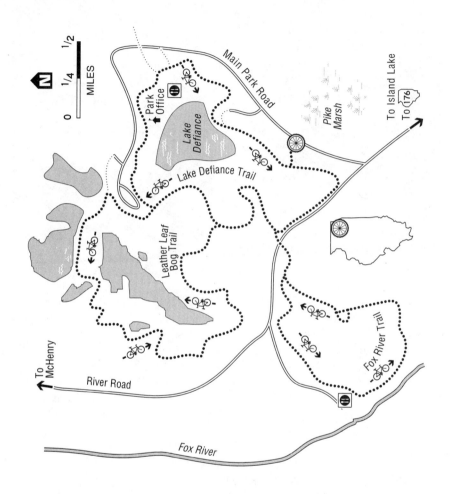

the man replied. The crushed limestone surface is wide and well maintained, but the area is fairly hilly. Three connecting loops comprise the ten miles of trails. The Fox River Trail is the flattest, and the Lake Defiance Trail and Leather Leaf Bog Trail are hillier.

You'll pass through a variety of terrains—lakes, woods, marshes, and prairies. By the marshes, get off your bike and spend a few minutes at one of the two viewing platforms observing the variety of waterfowl, including blue and

You don't have to go far from Chicago to cherish the solitude of a state park.

green herons, mallards, teals, and wood ducks. The trails are also home to fox, deer, mink, and beaver. In the vegetation department, look for marsh marigold, Saint-John's-wort, hoary willow, and other rare species. If you like to see battles between the plant and animal worlds, Pike Marsh, southeast of the Lake Defiance Trail, is home to one of the state's largest known colonies of pitcher plants, a rare species which traps and eats insects. If that makes you hungry, there are two concession stands in the park. Also, fishing and boat rentals are available. In short, Moraine Hills State Park is a great getaway not far from the Chicago area.

General location: Three miles south of McHenry, on River Road.
Elevation change: Elevation change is minimal; look for gently rolling hills.
Season: You can ride all year long, but the spring and fall are busier. I happen to like the smell of the lilacs and other wildflowers in the spring. The fall colors are pleasant, too.
Services: Water is available at the trailhead. All services are available in McHenry and Crystal Lake.
Hazards: Your main concern will be other trail users on pleasant days.
Rescue index: You're never too far from a parking lot. You'll find a phone at the park office and at McHenry Dam.
Land status: State park.
Maps: You can pick up a map at the park office or you can write Moraine Hills

State Park for one at the address below. The USGS 7.5 minute quad is Wauconda, with a small portion of the park falling into the McHenry quad.

Finding the trail: From IL 53 and US 12 (Rand Road), go west on US 12 for 12.5 miles to IL 176 (Liberty Street). Turn left on IL 176 and take that for 3.5 miles to River Road. Turn right on River Road and the entrance will be 2 miles on your right. Once in the park, drive up the main road to the Kettle Woods Day Use Area.

Sources of additional information:

Moraine Hills State Park
914 South River Road
McHenry, IL 60050
(815) 385-1624

Notes on the trail: You can begin your ride from the Kettle Woods Day Use Area. You'll see the trailhead from the lot. The one-way trails are color coded and have distance markers along the way.

RIDE 39 *DEER GROVE*

If you're north of Chicago, Deer Grove is where you should go to get some mountain bike action. While there is a paved bicycle trail in the forest preserve, the real excitement is on the cross-country ski trail. Even though this wide, 8.5-mile multiple-loop trail has paved sections, the majority of it is dirt. If you want even more exhilaration, you might explore the various dirt single-track spurs you'll find off the main trail. The single-track is narrower and hillier than the main trail. Your ride goes through dense woods full of rocks and fallen trees. Even though the Chicago area is notoriously flat, you'll be surprised by the elevation of this area. It's not uncommon to ride down a steep ravine, come to a creek crossing at the bottom, and hit a steep climb on the way back up. You'll also get to test your technical abilities in areas where you'll find jumps across streams. (The best riding of this type is found along the creek.)

With its variety of riding options, Deer Grove is good for the intermediate mountain biker looking for the moderate riding found along the ski trails or the expert mountain biker who wants to test his or her mettle on the single-track. As local area mountain biker Bart Dahlstrom puts it, "It's long enough to work up a good sweat without going around in circles."

General location: In Palatine, off Dundee Road.
Elevation change: The variation here is almost 100 feet.
Season: It's drier in the summer, so ride then if you don't mind the mosquitoes. The spring and fall can be wet and muddy.

RIDE 39 *DEER GROVE*

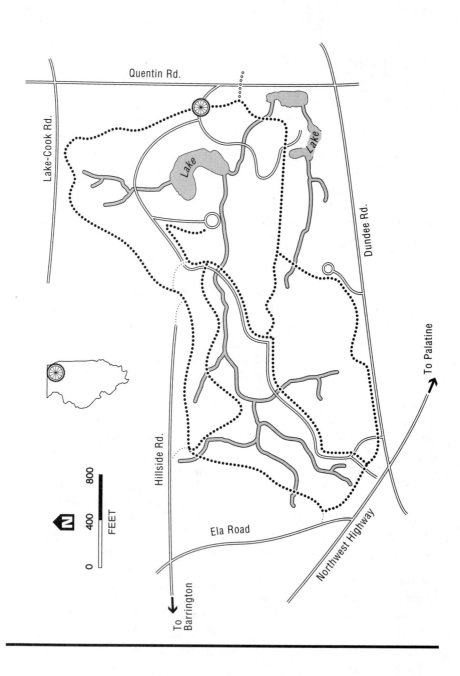

Services: Water is available at Deer Grove. All services are available in Palatine.
Hazards: You will find hikers on the main trail, so be cautious. The areas with the steep climbs are rocky and muddy.
Rescue index: The preserve gets a lot of use. The area is bounded by several busy roads as well.
Land status: Forest Preserve District of Cook County.
Maps: You can write the Forest Preserve District of Cook County at the address below for a map. There are also trail signs posted at the various parking areas. The USGS 7.5 minute quad for Deer Grove is Lake Zurich.
Finding the trail: From Interstate 90 and IL 53, go north on IL 53 for 5.5 miles to Dundee Road (IL 68). Turn left (west) on Dundee Road and go for 3 miles to Quentin Road. Turn right on Quentin Road and you'll see the entrance for Deer Grove half a mile on your left.

Sources of additional information:

Forest Preserve District of Cook County
536 North Harlem
River Forest, IL 60305
(312) 261-8400 (city)
(708) 366-9420 (suburbs)

Notes on the trail: You can park at any lot you come to, but you might wish to park at the first parking area and ride back a few yards to pick up the main trail where the trail map sign is.

The map does not show any of the spurs. As you ride the main trail, if a single-track spur looks inviting, get that exploring spirit. Most of the single-track spurs will connect back to the main trail.

The last I heard, the Cook County Forest Preserve District still had not formulated a policy on riding the single-track trails. You might wish to check their availability if you intend to depart from the main trail.

RIDE 40 *ELSEN'S HILL—WEST DUPAGE WOODS*

While there are only about four miles of trails through this upland oak woods, the area presents a few more challenges than the Regional Trail (see the next chapter). Located at one of the few fens in DuPage County, this trail has steeper grades especially toward the river. Elsen's Hill consists of three mowed grass loops, and occasionally you'll find gravel sections. The orange loop takes you along the meandering west branch of the DuPage River. If ponds are more your speed, stick to the green loop. The trail is easy since the forest preserve district keeps it clear and the trail wide. If horse use is heavy, the trails tend to have

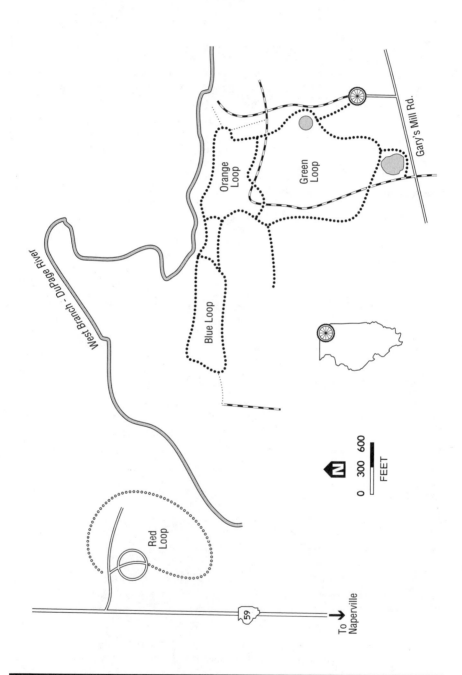

Pedaling down the wide double-track at the end of the Elsen's Hill trail.

severe indentations. Elsen's Hill is a good place to ride if you are interested in mountain biking but haven't had a lot of experience.

General location: Twenty-eight miles west of Chicago, near Winfield.

Elevation change: Total elevation change hovers around 60 feet.

Season: Ride here year-round, but in the late fall and early spring the rain can muddy the trail.

Services: Water is available at the forest preserve. All services are available in Warrenville, Wheaton, Naperville, and Lisle.

Hazards: There is a lot of horse traffic in the area, so remember your trail etiquette, should you pass an equestrian.

Rescue index: The area is fairly populated. You'll find a gas station at the corner of Winfield and Roosevelt Roads.

Land status: Forest Preserve District of DuPage County.

Maps: Maps are available at the Visitor Information signs located at the entrance to the trail. You can also write the Forest Preserve District at the address below.

Finding the trail: From Interstate 88 and IL 59, go north on IL 59 for 4 miles to Gary's Mill Road. The road itself is not marked, but there's a yellow intersection sign just before it. Turn right on Gary's Mill Road and you'll find the entrance just over a mile on your left.

Sources of additional information:

Forest Preserve District of DuPage County
P.O. Box 2339
Glen Ellyn, IL 60138
(708) 790-4900

Notes on the trail: The trail begins on the north end of the Elsen's Hill parking lot. Go up the service road from the lot past the rest rooms and turn left at the water pump. You can begin your ride there, or to the left of the pond. The trails are signed.

As always, please show respect if the trails are closed during wet weather.

RIDE 41 *REGIONAL TRAIL*

Jaunt—that's the perfect word to describe the Regional Trail. Neither technical nor taxing, this ride carries you along a wide, multi-purpose, limestone gravel path. The Regional Trail itself is about 7.5 miles one-way (15 miles total), but when you add in the spur loops in the 3 forest preserves it crosses, your total ride comes to a little over 16 miles. The Forest Preserve District of DuPage County does an excellent job maintaining its trails and takes great pride in them. As I rode with one of the Sector Managers, Mike Palazzetti, he enthusiastically pointed out to me where edges of the trail had been cleared and diversion ditches had been dug. In fact, he even stopped to give an erosion explanation to a group of riders who had strayed off the trail. He has a lot to be proud of: on the fringes of the suburban Chicago area, this trail passes through oak woodlands, open meadows, marshes, rivers, lakes, wetlands, and prairies in the Blackwell, Herrick Lake, and Danada Forest Preserves.

In the Blackwell Forest Preserve on the northernmost section of the Regional Trail, you can branch off and ride the intersecting loops of the Catbird, Nighthawk, and Bob-O-Link Trails. These three grass trails circle McKee Marsh and give you a bumpier ride than the Regional Trail. If you're a casual rider taking the family out for a stroll, you might wish to bypass these trails, but most mountain bikers will find them easy. McKee Marsh, by the way, was the site where the skeleton of a woolly mammoth was excavated.

As the Regional Trail makes its way into the Herrick Forest Preserve, it becomes part of three intersecting loops: Meadowlark Trail, Green Heron Trail, and Bluebird Trail. The loops, like the Regional Trail, are limestone gravel and provide a quiet ride through prairies, woodlands, and especially wetlands. Perhaps you'll spot egrets munching on tadpoles in the cattail marsh in the middle of the Green Heron Trail loop.

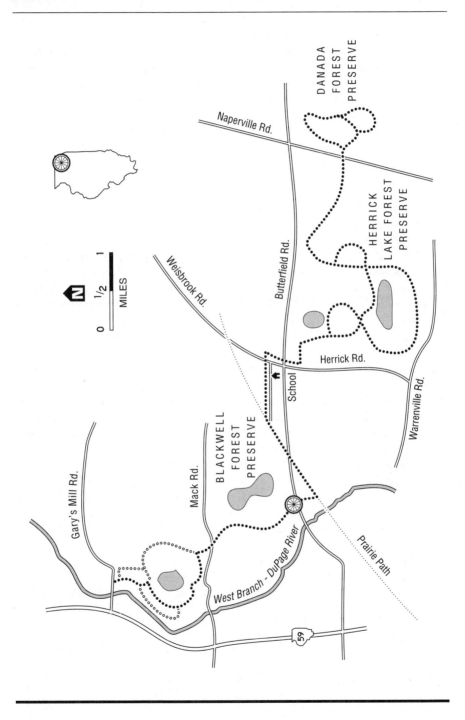

DANADA FOREST PRESERVE

Naperville Rd.

HERRICK LAKE FOREST PRESERVE

Butterfield Rd.

Weisbrook Rd.

N

0   1/2   1

MILES

Herrick Rd.

School

Warrenville Rd.

Gary's Mill Rd.

Mack Rd.

BLACKWELL FOREST PRESERVE

West Branch - DuPage River

Prairie Path

59

The final leg of the Regional Trail goes through Danada Forest Preserve and passes by a Kentucky-style equestrian center. At the eastern end of the Regional Trail, the one-mile, double-loop Nature Trail gives you a slightly different feel than the main trail. Still crushed limestone, the Nature Trail is a little narrower and does not have mowed borders. Curving through an open savanna, you'll pass many beautiful wildflowers in the summer—columbine, spring beauty, shooting stars, and toothwort among them.

Even though you're in the Chicago suburbs, the area doesn't lack for variety of animals: coyotes, foxes, weasels, painted turtles, leopard frogs, owls, hawks, bob-o-links, meadowlarks, orioles, egrets, and great blue herons. All in all, this easy ride is fun for the entire family and makes for a pleasant diversion from the commotion of our busy lives.

General location: Twenty-nine miles west of Chicago near Warrenville, off IL 59 and IL 56.

Elevation change: Negligible.

Season: Ride the Regional Trail year-round. Late fall and early spring can produce a lot of rain, so you might want to avoid the grass trails at Blackwell then.

Services: Water can be found by Silver Lake in Blackwell, by Herrick Lake, and near Danada Mansion in Danada. There are telephones by the entrance to Blackwell and in a few spots by Herrick Lake and Danada. There are even concession stands open during the summer in Blackwell and Herrick Lake. All services are available in Warrenville, Wheaton, Naperville, and Lisle.

Hazards: The only hazards present on this trail are other cyclists, hikers, and equestrians.

Rescue index: The trails are heavily used and bounded by several major roads. You can also find help at the 2 guard residences, the concession area, and the shop complexes at Blackwell; at the guard residence and the concession stand at Herrick Lake; and at the 2 guard residences at Danada.

Land status: Forest Preserve District of DuPage County.

Maps: You can pick up maps of the forest preserves at the Visitor Information signs in the various parking areas. You can also write to the Forest Preserve District of DuPage County to get copies. The USGS 7.5 minute quads for this area are Naperville and Wheaton, but the maps from the Forest Preserve District will be sufficient.

Finding the trail: From Interstate 88, go north on IL 59 for 1.2 miles to Butterfield Road. Turn right (east), and in 1.5 miles, you'll see the entrance for Blackwell on your left. As you pull in, the parking area is just off to your right.

Sources of additional information:

Forest Preserve District of DuPage County
P.O. Box 2339
Glen Ellyn, IL 60138
(708) 790-4900

Duane and Mike glide easily down the well-maintained Regional Trail.

Notes on the trail: The Blackwell Forest Preserve trailhead isn't at the beginning of the trail, but this provides a good place to park. (You can park, if you wish, at Herrick or Danada and begin your ride from there.) From the parking area, you can access the Herrick and Danada portions of the trail by riding out the way you came in and crossing to the other side of Butterfield Road. You'll see an opening through the bushes that will connect you with Prairie Path. Turn left on Prairie Path. (The path will put you on a few streets, but you'll be able to follow the route.) Follow Prairie Path until you spot a school. Cut through the school lot to get to the next street (Weisbrook Road). Turn right on Weisbrook and go one block to Butterfield Road. (South of Butterfield Road, Weisbrook Road turns into Herrick Road.) At the southeast corner of the intersection, you'll see where the trail picks up in Herrick Lake Forest Preserve. As you follow the trail through Herrick, you'll come to several intersections where you can turn off on Meadowlark Trail, Green Heron Trail, or Bluebird Trail. Take whatever options you fancy or ride straight through into Danada Forest Preserve. Once in Danada, you'll pass by the exercise track before riding under Naperville Road. If you ride through the parking area and past the barns, you'll come to the last quarter mile of the Regional Trail and the one-mile Nature Trail.

After you return to the Blackwell Forest Preserve parking lot, you'll see where the Regional Trail picks up on the west side of the parking area. As you ride that portion, you'll cross Mack Road. About a quarter mile later, you'll come to the grass trails of Nighthawk, Catbird, and Bob-O-Link. Branch off on these trails or continue on the Regional Trail. When you hit Gary's Mill Road on the north, you've reached the end of the ride.

This trail also connects up with Prairie Path.

RIDE 42 *WATERFALL GLEN*

You'll love this scenic, eight-and-a-half-mile loop. Period. One of the most popular multi-purpose trails in the western Chicago suburbs, it passes through a variety of terrains, including meadows, praries, woodlands, and wetlands. While the entire forest preserve surrounds Argonne National Laboratory, a major scientific installation, you never really see it. The eight-foot-wide gravel trail is suitable for all ages and abilities. This is the perfect place to get away from the flurry of your daily life and spend some time on a leisurely ride. Few technical skills are required, so you could fly down the trail—but why would you want to? Relax on this trail.

The forest preserve contains several sites of note. The county's only artesian well is at the south end of the preserve. You'll pass through the "leaning forest," an area where a 1976 tornado bowed the trees. For a scenic view, look across the Des Plaines River at the town of Lemont nestled in the hills. You may spot many species of animals, including coyotes, beavers, bluebirds, herons, and cranes. But the animal you want to keep your eyes peeled for is the deer. I don't mean your average, everyday, brown-colored deer, but a species of white deer. Not a genetic mutation caused by Argonne National Laboratory, these white fallow deer were actually imported here from Asia at the turn of the century. Oh, and one more thing. With a name like Waterfall Glen, you'd expect to see a waterfall—and there is one. Oddly enough, though, the waterfall has nothing to do with the name of the preserve. The area was named after Seymour "Bud" Waterfall, an early forest preserve district president.

General location: Off Cass Avenue, south of Interstate 55 in Darien.
Elevation change: Negligible. The only small hill is by Saw Mill Creek.
Season: Enjoy the changes year-round. The autumn colors are especially vivid.
Services: Water and restrooms are available at the trailhead. All services can be found in Downers Grove or Willow Springs.
Hazards: Since this is a popular multi-purpose trail, you'll be sharing the path with both pedestrians and equestrians. Especially watch the traffic crossing Cass Avenue.
Rescue index: The ranger station often isn't manned, but Lemont Road to the west of the preserve and Cass Avenue to the east are quite busy. Also, there's a guard booth for Argonne National Laboratory near the trailhead. You

RIDE 42 *WATERFALL GLEN*

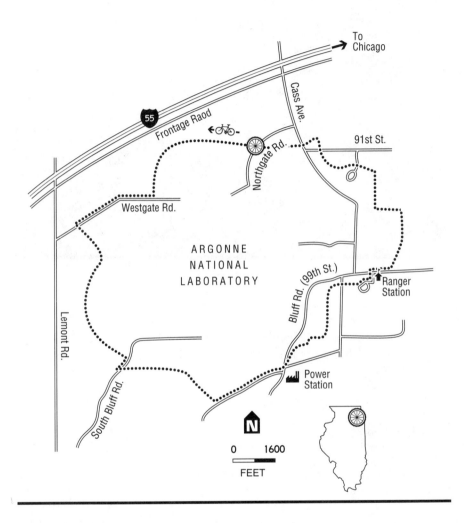

probabably don't want to bother the lab, but in an emergency, would they turn you away?

Land status: Forest Preserve District of DuPage County.

Maps: The Forest Preserve District has a great colored map which is sufficient for your needs. You can write for one at the address below. Also, maps are available at the information sign at the trailhead. The USGS 7.5 minute quad is mostly Sag Bridge with a bit found in the Romeoville quad.

Savoring a quiet ride down the popular Waterfall Glen trail.

Finding the trail: From I-55, take the Cass Avenue south exit. Go south on Cass Avenue a quarter mile and turn right on Northgate Road. Go to the second entrance labeled "Waterfall Glen—Ski Equestrian Trailhead Area." The trail begins at the south end of the parking lot to the left of the restrooms.

Sources of additional information:

> Forest Preserve District of DuPage County
> P.O. Box 2339
> Glen Ellyn, IL 60138
> (708) 790-4900

Notes on the trail: Since the area has had trail usage conflicts in the past, please stay on the main trail marked by brown carsonite posts with a white circle. Don't take any user-made, single-track spurs you might find. Following the trail is easy, except in a few spots: By Westgate Road, you'll need to ride down the road a little, and the trail will continue again off to your left. Later, when you get to the power station, turn left down the road; the trail will pick up on your right in a few yards. Finally, just past the ranger station, the trail has not been graveled. When it becomes dirt, you'll enter a clearing. The markings aren't clear here, so look carefully for another clearing on your left, heading west, where you will want to turn. This stretch is a little rough from horse use, but it will be well worth it when you come to a majestic wetland area, where I've even seen a sparrow chasing a 6-foot crane. Only in the Chicago area!

RIDE 43 *SWALLOW CLIFF WOODS*

This trail has two personalities. If you follow the main gravel loop only, about a seven-mile trip, you'll ride along a wide, quiet trail used by joggers, hikers, and equestrians. However, if you get off the main trail and onto any of the dirt single-track, you're in for a wild ride. In fact, Andy Pliska, a local mountain biker, is thrilled by the single-track riding. "I've explored the trails out West," he says, "but you can't beat this area for being right outside a major metropolitan area. This is a surprisingly technical trail for the Midwest." The single-track is fast and challenging. You're always encountering obstacles ranging from fallen trees and stumps to ditches and rocks. There's even a major ravine right off 104th Avenue. Both the main trail and the single-track spurs have moderate climbs where the grade is slight. The spur trails have a few uphill switchbacks as well. You'll find stream crossings on the main trail and the spurs. If you're a novice rider, you can easily get across the water if you don't wish to ride through it. (Of course, I rode before work one time and forgot to bring a change of socks. The result: suit, tie, and bare feet in the office.)

The woods along the trail contain sycamores, large ironwood trees, and white pines, as well as blackberry, dewberry, and raspberry patches in meadow areas. Also, if you ride in the winter, bring a sled for the toboggan slide, the longest and highest in the Chicago region. Without a doubt, riders of all abilities will flock to this area. Sunday riders will enjoy following the main trail, tested occasionally by a few small hills and short water crossings. The more advanced riders will get the added bonus of exploring the technical, single-track spurs.

General location: At the Palos Forest Preserve off IL 83, half a mile west of US 45.

Elevation change: The overall elevation gain is about 150 feet. Not bad for suburban Chicago, huh?

Season: Ride all year long. In the winter, bring that toboggan. In the fall, head out to the Great Pumpkin Smash Off-Road Rally, sponsored by Wheel Thing.

Services: Water is available at the trailhead. Many of the surrounding suburbs have all services, including LaGrange and Orland Park.

Hazards: On the main trail, be prepared to contend with horses and hikers. Also, be careful when crossing the 2 major intersections. On the spurs, the obstacles could trip you up.

Rescue index: You're never far from a major road if you need help.

Land status: Forest Preserve District of Cook County.

Maps: The Forest Preserve District can send you a map depicting the main trail and several of the picnic areas and sites along the way. Write to the address

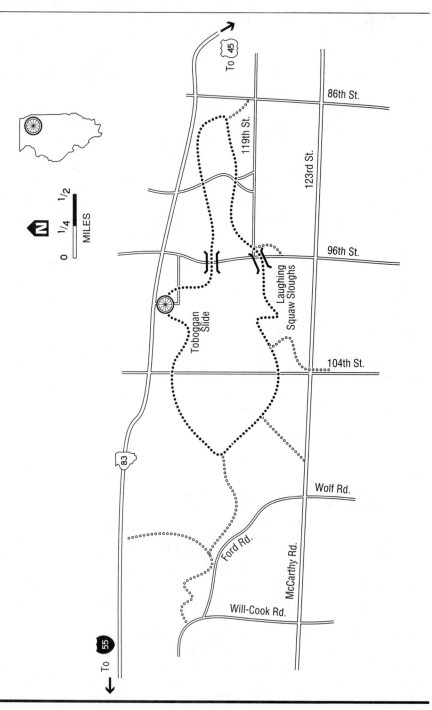

To 45

86th St.

119th St.

123rd St.

96th St.

Laughing Squaw Sloughs

Toboggan Slide

104th St.

83

Wolf Rd.

Ford Rd.

McCarthy Rd.

Will-Cook Rd.

55

To

N

0   1/4   1/2

MILES

Riders of all abilities find a home at Swallow Cliff woods.

below. If you feel you need them, the USGS 7.5 minute quads for this area are Palos Park and Sag Bridge.

Finding the trail: From the north: From Interstate 55 and LaGrange Road (US 45), take LaGrange Road south for 5.5 miles to IL 83. Exit at IL 83 and turn left off the exit ramp. Go down IL 83 for a half mile to the Swallow Cliff Toboggan Slide. You can park in this lot.

From the south: From I-55 and IL 83, take IL 83 south for 7.5 miles to the Swallow Cliff Toboggan Slide.

Sources of additional information:

> Forest Preserve District of Cook County
> 536 North Harlem Avenue
> River Forest, IL 60305
> (312) 261-8400 (city)
> (708) 366-9420 (suburban)

> Wheel Thing
> 15 South LaGrange Road
> LaGrange, IL 60525
> (708) 352-3822

Notes on the trail: You can begin the ride at the parking area entrance where the trail crosses the access road. Start in whichever direction you like. The main trail is not difficult to follow. The map does not show any of the spurs, so as you ride the main trail and find single-track worth checking out, go for it. Most of the single track spurs will connect back to the main trail.

The Maple Lake Trail is also accessible from the Swallow Cliff Trail by riding north on 104th Avenue.

The last I heard, the Cook County Forest Preserve District still had not formulated a policy on riding the single-track trails. You might wish to check their availability if you plan on departing from the main trail.

RIDE 44 *MAPLE LAKE*

One person's algae is another's slough. This 12-mile loop is a little longer and slightly more difficult than the Swallow Cliff loop. It passes around six sloughs and a couple of lakes. Several other sloughs dot this forest preserve. These wetland areas are home to numerous waterfowl, including ducks, geese, and egrets. Traveling through woods and meadows, this gravelly multi-purpose trail features a wide path with few obstacles, making it a pleasant ride for the entire family. Like Swallow Cliffs, you will find single-track spurs departing from the main trail. In general, the single-track here is a little easier than the single-track at Swallow Cliffs.

Several attractions also make this an ideal family recreation spot. In addition to picnicking, you can fish at Bullfrog Lake and at Maple Lake, the site where, as a child, I once hooked the back of my shirt. If the kids don't want to fish, they can scour the banks for bullfrogs and crawdads. Boat rentals are also available at Maple Lake. Another attraction is the Little Red Schoolhouse, a nature center near Longjohn Slough containing indoor exhibits and native animals. Also, on the southwest corner of the trail is the site of the first Argonne Laboratory, where nuclear fuel from the original Manhattan Project is buried. Spent fuel aside, this is a great spot to visit if you want a simple, peaceful ride only minutes from one of the largest urban areas in the country.

General location: At Palos Forest Preserve off IL 83, 3 miles west of US 45.
Elevation change: Surprisingly, you'll find 120 feet of elevation change here.
Season: Ride here year-round. Summer is crowded; the fall colors are pleasing in October.
Services: Water is available at the trailhead. All services are available in LaGrange and Orland Park.
Hazards: The trail is popular with equestrians and hikers. Be careful crossing the streets.
Rescue index: The trail is well traveled and crosses several major roads.

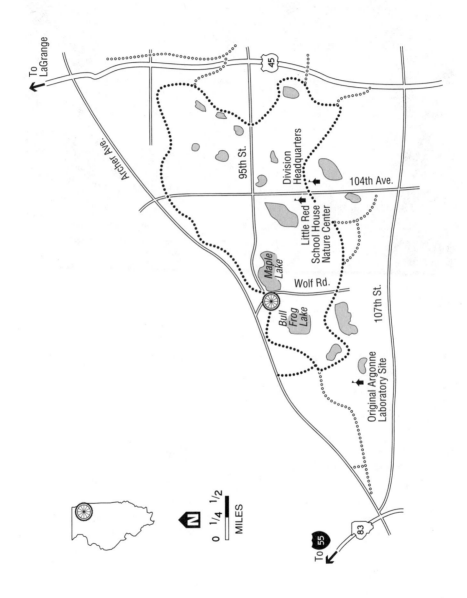

Dotted with several sloughs, Maple Lake provides riders a "nature break" not far from Chicago.

Land status: Forest Preserve District of Cook County.

Maps: The Forest Preserve District can send you a map of the main trail and several of the attractions. Write to the address below. The USGS 7.5 minute quads for this area are Palos Park and Sag Bridge.

Finding the trail: From the north: From Interstate 55 and LaGrange Road (US 45), take LaGrange Road south 1 mile to Archer Avenue (IL 171). Go south on Archer Avenue 3 miles to 95th Street. (Look for the Maple Lake sign.) Turn left and stay to the right, hooking up with Wolf Road in just .3 mile. The parking area is on your right for Maple Lake West and Bullfrog Lake.

From the south: From I-55 and IL 83, take IL 83 south for 3 miles to Archer Avenue (IL 171). Turn left and go 2.5 miles to 95th Street. (Look for two yellow intersection signs to help you locate 95th Street.) Turn right and stay to the right, hooking up with Wolf Road in just .2 mile. The parking area is on your right for Maple Lake West and Bullfrog Lake.

Sources of additional information:

Forest Preserve District of Cook County
536 North Harlem Avenue
River Forest, IL 60305
(312) 261-8400 (city)
(708) 366-9420 (suburban)

Wheel Thing
15 South LaGrange Road
LaGrange, IL 60525
(708) 352-3822

Notes on the trail: You can pick up the trail from the north side of the parking lot. Pass through the picnic area and you will run into the trail. You can go left or right. The single-track spurs are not depicted on the map of the main trail.

The Swallow Cliff Trail is also accessible from Maple Lake Trail by riding south on 104th Avenue.

The last I heard, the Cook County Forest Preserve District still had not formulated a policy on riding the single-track trails. You might wish to check their availability if you plan on departing from the main trail.

RIDE 45 *HAMMEL WOODS*

Hammel Woods is the quintessential suburban forest preserve: a small area used for recreational groups, popular with weekend and after-work joggers. Don't be deterred by the fact that this trail is a short three miles. This figure eight with a connecting spur is a great place for a quick aerobic workout—take as many laps as you like. In fact, I use Hammel Woods for my training rides. It's popular with the Joliet Bicycle Club because of the short but steep uphill and downhill at a bridged stream crossing.

The primarily dirt trail is wide, so you won't need a lot of technical skills. The eastern side of the northern loop does have some blind curves and the surface is rooted—a good place to practice bike handling techniques. Hammerheads may wish to tackle a few very narrow, unmarked spurs, many of which lead nowhere and are steep, rocky, and treacherous. As you pedal through the woods, keep an eye out for the occasional deer and the flit of a scarlet tanager.

General location: In Joliet, northwest of I-55 and IL 52.
Elevation change: The one steep hill doesn't significantly affect the elevation.
Season: Ride this one all year long, but carry mosquito repellent in the summer at dusk.
Services: Water and restrooms can be found at the picnic groves. All services can be found in Joliet. For bike service, try Al's Bike Shop in Joliet.
Hazards: Keep an eye out for pedestrians out for a jog or a leisurely stroll. You will need to pay attention on the one major hill as the steep trail runs alongside a metal stairway.
Rescue index: Since the area is small, you're never far from a major road. Black Road, IL 59, and IL 52 are all major thoroughfares.

RIDE 45 *HAMMEL WOODS*

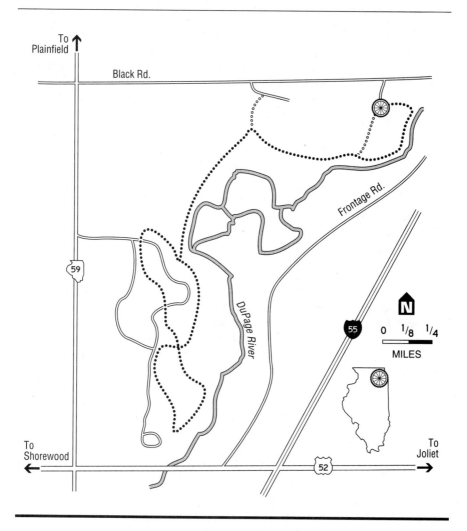

Land status: Forest Preserve District of Will County.

Maps: You can get a map from the Will County Forest Preserve District at the address below. The USGS 7.5 minute quad for this area is Plainfield.

Finding the trail: From I-55, take IL 52 west to the first stop light, IL 59 (Brook Forest Avenue). Turn right (north) on IL 59. Pass up the entrance on IL 59 and go to the next stop light, Black Road. Turn right on Black Road, heading east a short distance. Pass the first entrance to Hammel Woods and take the second

Mark practices his climbing technique on Hammel Wood's uphill climb.

entrance a few yards further. The brown carsonite sign marking the trail entrance is east of the soccer field.

Sources of additional information:

> Will County Forest Preserve District Office
> 22606 South Cherry Hill Road
> Joliet, IL 60433
> (815) 727-8700

> Ski and Bike Chalet
> I-55 and IL 52
> Shorewood, IL 60431
> (815) 741-4456

Notes on the trail: Beginning at the DuPage River Access spur will insure that you hit the steep hill. As you start off, the grass portion of the trail will flank the fields along the DuPage River before heading into the forest. After you travel alongside the Crumby Recreation Area and over 2 small wooden crossways, you'll come to a point where you will see a small shelter ahead of you. The main trail will veer to the right. Soon, you'll come to the stairway heading down. Keep to the left of the stairs. At the top of the hill on the other side, go left or right to enter the figure-eight loops.

Rockford

Rockford is the second largest city in the state, and the two trails listed here represent the northernmost rides in this guide. The original prairies here have mostly disappeared, as have the forests, but reforestation, as well as prairie and wetland restoration efforts, have created a few pockets of natural areas similar to the original landscape.

Two rides, one north and one south of Rockford, will give you a chance to enjoy some mountain biking. While neither trail is difficult, you'll enjoy the scenery they provide. Rockford may be well populated, but Rock Cut State Park and Blackhawk Springs Forest Preserve are great places to come for a little R&R.

Rest and relaxation is one way to look at it. You could make a case for the opposite—you can "take it hard" if you like and give yourself a workout, too. Rock Cut State Park, with its wide, maintained trails, is a good place for an aerobic ride. The same is true for Blackhawk Springs Forest Preserve. The main trail here follows the Kishwaukee River and can be fun when ridden fast. Not everything here in Rockford, though, lacks technical challenge. There are areas in Blackhawk Springs which will make you slow up a bit—unless you like getting hit in the head by a branch.

Thanks to Tom Hutten, who helped supply information for Rock Cut State Park.

RIDE 46 *ROCK CUT STATE PARK*

Come to Rock Cut to cycle, and stay for the swimming, boating, and fishing. There are ten miles of trails at Rock Cut, seven of which are open to mountain bikers—the cross-country ski trails. The mostly dirt trails are well maintained; in the winter months, park workers clear the trails for the cross-country skiers. Leave most of your technical skills at home, but bring along the ones that help you avoid hikers.

This loop trail offers a shorter connecting loop to the northeast. You're not likely to get lost on this ride, but often the trail runs parallel to some of the trails designated strictly for hikers, so pay attention. Your endurance won't be challenged here; the few climbs are neither hard nor steep, just long—and that's long by Illinois standards, so don't sweat it. As you ride, keep an eye out for wild turkey, deer, fox, and beaver. The spring and summer showcase over 100 types of wildflowers.

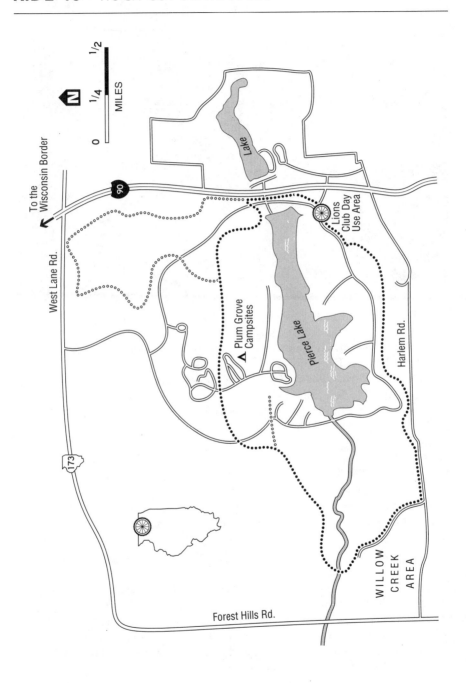

To the
Wisconsin Border

West Lane Rd.

90

173

N

MILES

0   1/4   1/2

Lake

Lions
Club Day
Use Area

Harlem Rd.

Plum Grove
Campsites

Pierce Lake

WILLOW
CREEK
AREA

Forest Hills Rd.

Tom hits a gradual uphill on the cross-country ski trails at popular Rock Cut State Park.

General location: In Caledonia, just northeast of Rockford.

Elevation change: The climbs are slight.

Season: Ride all year, but the fall is nice when the colors are out, the trails are drier, and the air is less humid.

Services: Water, camping, and concessions are found in the park. For bike service, try Kegel's Bike Shop in Rockford.

Hazards: If you're picking up speed, be careful of roots and especially hikers or other cyclists.

Rescue index: The park is usually well populated. There are phones by the boat launch and the swimming lake.

Land status: State park.

Maps: The map available at the park office or the main concession stand will suit your needs. You can also write the park at the address below. The main USGS 7.5 minute quad is Caledonia, with a small portion found on the Rockford North quad map.

Finding the trail: From Interstate 90, take the East Riverside Boulevard exit. Go left. At the first stop light, turn right at McFarland road. Go a short way to the end of the road where it Ts and turn right. Shortly after you cross back over I-90, you'll see the entrance on your left. Once you're in the park, turn left at the first stop sign. Go for just a bit and turn left again. Take this road to the Lions Club Day Use Area and park your vehicle.

Sources of additional information:

Rock Cut State Park
7318 Harlem Road
Caledonia, IL 61011
(815) 885-3311

Kegel's Bike Shop
2605 Charles Street
Rockford, IL 61108
(815) 229-5826

Notes on the trail: From the parking area, turn right onto the road; go a few yards down, and the entrance to the trail will be on your left (look for the cross-walk). When you get to the Willow Creek area, you'll come to a gravel stretch. Turn right onto the gravel; then you'll see a sign where the grass trail picks up on your left. Cross a quaint bridge, and soon you'll come to a Y intersection. Take the left trail. You'll pass through a valley, followed by a mild climb with a nice view of the tree ridge in the distance. After a fun little downhill section, you'll come to another uphill—not difficult, just long. At the top of the hill, you'll come to a road; turn left, and a few hundred feet further turn right onto the trail again. After you pass the Plum Grove campsites, you'll have the option of taking a loop to your left if you want to add a little more mileage to your ride; otherwise, keep going straight. After you cross a road, you'll see 2 parallel trails. Take the trail on your right, and soon you'll be riding parallel with I-90, followed by another fun downhill. When you come to the next road, turn left, and that road will take you back to your vehicle.

Remember to ride only on the trails posted with bicycle symbols. When you don't see a bicycle symbol, you can follow the cross-country ski signs. Park officials request that you not ride when the trails are wet or covered with 2 or more inches of snow.

RIDE 47 *BLACKHAWK SPRINGS FOREST PRESERVE*

Ride this one fast for a workout or slow for a scenic ride along the Kishwaukee River. Either pace will be enjoyable along this seven-mile each way, out-and-back trail passing through marshes and forest. The main dirt trail is wide and offers little technical challenge, making this a ride suitable for those who have lesser technical skills. The trail is smooth and rolling, and since you probably won't find a lot of people in your way, make it aerobic. If you're looking for a

RIDE 47 *BLACKHAWK SPRINGS FOREST PRESERVE*

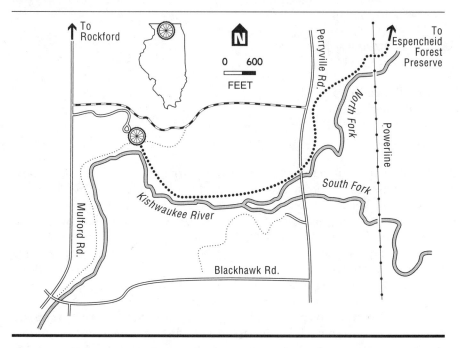

more technically challenging ride, split off from the main trail and follow one of the narrower single-track spurs. The spurs are rockier and give you opportunities to duck under branches and maneuver your way over roots.

Near the end of the trail, you'll find a small quarry pit where ATVs commonly ride. If you like, head into the pit area and romp around yourself. Most of the ride is along the river, so you might see deer and raccoon making their way to the banks for a drink. Several bird species call Blackhawk Springs their home, including hooded warblers, broad-winged hawks, Acadian flycatchers, and veeries.

General location: Three miles southeast of the Rockford city limits on Mulford Road.

Elevation change: The few hills are not steep, and you'll find no more than 100 feet of elevation change.

Season: Early summer to late fall is best. The area is too muddy in the early spring, when the river is high.

Services: Water is available at the trailhead. All services are available in Rockford. The folks over at Kegel's Bike Shop will be most helpful.

Hazards: The ride is pretty mellow. Just use a little caution on stretches that parallel the river. On the single-track, watch for the low-hanging branches.

Rescue index: You're only a few miles outside the city limits, so the area is fairly populated, and you're never far from roads where you could get to a residence.

Land status: Winnebago County Forest Preserve.

Maps: You can get a simple map from the Forest Preserve by writing to the address below. The USGS 7.5 minute quad for this area is Cherry Valley.

Finding the trail: From Interstate 90, take the US 20 bypass for roughly 4 miles to the Perryville Road exit. Go south on Perryville Road about 1 mile to Linden Road. Go left on Linden about 1.5 miles and turn left on Mulford Road. Go south on Mulford about 2.5 miles. Blackhawk Forest Preserve is on the left.

Sources of additional information:

Winnebago County Forest Preserve District
5500 Northrock Drive
Rockford, IL 61103
(815) 877-6100

Kegel's Bike Shop
2605 Charles Street
Rockford, IL 61108
(815) 229-5826

Notes on the trail: The ride begins at the back of the parking lot by the outhouses. The trail leaves Blackhawk Springs Forest Preserve and enters Espencheid Forest Preserve. Keep going if you desire. The single-track spurs branching from the main trail eventually make their way back. These spurs are not depicted on the map of the main trail.

Peoria

What happens when you combine the Illinois River with a rich agricultural basin? You get Peoria, Illinois. And you also get some wonderful areas to mountain bike. Early French settlers in the area probably didn't have mountain biking on their minds when they erected Fort Crevecoeur, the first foreign fort in Illinois, but those of us who followed can appreciate the unique terrain here. Local mountain biker Troy Pritchard keeps it in perspective: "The terrain has a mixture of the southern and northern parts of the state."

That variety shows up in the trails. With the exception of the easy Rock Island Trail, the rest provide a mix of riding experiences. I would be remiss if I didn't make special mention of Jubilee College State Park, perhaps one of the best intermediate-level trails around. In all, Peoria is rich in mountain biking opportunities. "There's a lot to offer in this area that people don't know about," says Troy. "There may be other trail areas that we don't even know about."

Mountain biking. Will it play in Peoria? You bet.

Thanks to Troy for supplying information on some of his favorite rides.

RIDE 48 *ROCK ISLAND TRAIL*

This popular multi-purpose trail follows the abandoned Rock Island Railroad line between Alta and Toulon. Spanning 26 miles one-way (52 miles total), this crushed limestone trail is the perfect place to take the family for an easy weekend ride. The tree-lined trail makes its way through farmlands, prairie grass, and wildflowers. The best spot to see the prairie as it was years ago is between the Peoria and Stark county lines. You'll also ride over a couple of nice bridges, the most interesting being a trestle bridge crossing the Spoon River between Wyoming and Toulon. Make sure you stop for refreshments in the five towns through which the trail passes: Alta, Dunlap, Princeville, Wyoming, and Toulon. After all, you won't want to rush this ride.

General location: The Rock Island Trail begins in the town of Alta and ends in Toulon.
Elevation change: Negligible.
Season: This trail can be ridden year-round. You'll especially enjoy the changing colors in autumn; bring your cross-country skis in the winter.
Services: Services are available in the 5 towns along the way. The folks at Russell's Cycle World in Washington will be most helpful with bike service.

RIDE 48 *ROCK ISLAND TRAIL*

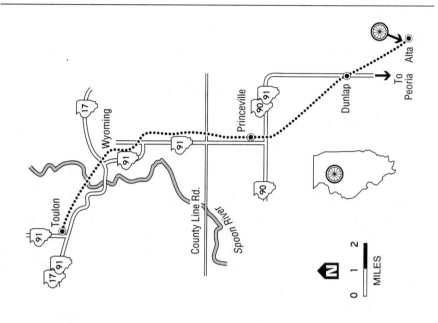

Hazards: Watch for other trail users during nice weather. Also, use caution at street crossings.

Rescue index: The trail is widely used, and you'll cross many streets where you can flag down traffic.

Land status: Illinois state park.

Maps: You can write Rock Island State Park for a brochure map at the address below. The USGS 7.5 minute quads for this area are Dunlap, Edelstein, Princeville, and Wyoming.

Finding the trail: In Peoria, Interstate 74 hooks up with IL 88. Take IL 88 north, and go 5 miles from the edge of the city limits to Alta Road. Go west on Alta Road less than a mile; when you get into the town of Alta, follow the signs to the trail. From the parking area, you'll see the trailhead.

Contact Rock Island Trail State Park for additional places to pick up the trail.

Sources of additional information:

Rock Island Trail State Park
P.O. Box 64
Wyoming, IL 61491
(309) 695-2228

Russell's Cycle World
308 North Main
Washington, IL 61571
(309) 444-2098

Notes on the trail: The trail is easy to follow. When you pass through the towns, directional signs will point the way along streets and sidewalks.

RIDE 49 *JUBILEE COLLEGE STATE PARK*

"Fun" is how Derrick Moscardelli, an IMBA/RIDE coordinator, describes this area. I agree. The day I rode here, we assembled an ad hoc group of riders from the local area, as well as Springfield, Joliet, Chicago, and even as far away as Iowa. Everyone had varying degrees of experience, but all concluded this was some of the best riding around. There are over 40 miles of dirt and grass loop trails at Jubilee, about 80% of which are open to mountain bikes. The area has the right mix of uphill riding, downhill riding, and best of all, gully crossings, some of which retain water. The gullies will challenge your bike handling skills, but if you're not feeling daring, you could walk around them.

The creek crossings have bridges without railings, so take care as you wind around the trails and come upon one—especially in the winter when the bridges might be slick. (Of course, it was summer when your humble author missed a bridge and ended up in the briars: "I'm okay! Really, I'm okay!") The trails are wide and well maintained, so you won't have to worry much about deadfall, rocks, and the like; it's those wonderful gullies that require your attention. Some of the grassy areas of the trail are a little rough, but not enough to cause you concern.

General location: Off Interstate 74 in Brimfield, slightly northwest of Peoria.
Elevation change: The hills roll along, but the overall elevation change is no more than about 100 feet.
Season: The autumn colors make a nice backdrop for this ride.
Services: The parking area has water. Food and lodging are available in Kickapoo. All services are available in Peoria. For bike service, visit Russell's Cycle World in Washington.
Hazards: Use your bike handling skills to navigate the gullies, of course, but also be careful about hammerheading too fast around a curve and coming upon a hiker.
Rescue index: There is a phone in the parking area by the maintenance shop. From the picnic areas, you can follow the access roads out to the main road.
Land status: Illinois state park.

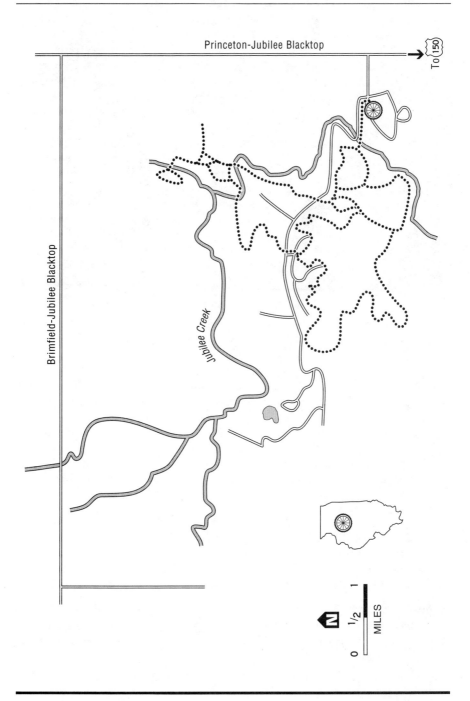

You'll find some of the best mountain biking in the state at Jubilee College State Park.

Maps: A topographical map is available from Jubilee College State Park. Write for one at the address below. The USGS 7.5 minute quad is Oak Hill.
Finding the trail: From I-74, take Exit 82, Kickapoo/Edwards Road, north. A mile later, turn left at US 150. Another mile later, turn right at the Princeville-Jubilee blacktop. Go 2 miles and turn left on Jubilee College Road, which will take you into the entrance.

Sources of additional information:

Jubilee College State Park
13921 West Route 150
Brimfield, IL 61517
(309) 446-3758

Russell's Cycle World
308 North Main
Washington, IL 61571
(309) 444-2098

Notes on the trail: From the parking area, go back up the road you came in. Just outside the entrance, turn left up the road. You'll see the entrance to the trail on your left just before a 15 mph speed limit sign. Look for the trail between the trees.

These trails can be twice as fun on a tandem mountain bike.

When you're on the trail, the first sign you come to will have an arrow pointing to the right, but keep going straight on a narrow single-track. When you come to an intersection with a cross-country ski sign, go left. You'll ride through a grassy area before you enter the woods again. At a trail map sign, veer to your left. At the next cross-country ski–signed intersection, go right. You'll go straight across 2 picnic areas. After the second one, take the trail to your right. You'll ride down a hill, across a bridge, and back uphill again. At the top, hang a right at the trail map. Soon you'll come to a wide clearing; turn left and ride up the clearing. Turn right at the next trail map. The next intersection has left, soft right, and hard right options. Take the soft right. And at the next intersection, follow the ski route trail to the left. After another grassy area, you'll enter the woods again. Take the trail to the right. You'll come to another intersecting trail. Turn left, and from here you should be able to retrace the way you came in.

It's easy to get turned around, so allow time to get lost. You can get your bearings from any of the signs posted throughout the trail. When all else fails, you can take one of the picnic area access roads back out to the main road.

RIDE 50 *PIMITEOUI TRAIL*

Located on the outskirts of Peoria, the Pimiteoui Trail begins as a smooth, flat ride along the Illinois River. Despite the fact that it begins in an industrial area, the trail along the river is rather scenic. You'll travel about five miles one way on a wide path, and then you'll need to ride roughly seven miles through a paved residential area before continuing again in Detweiller Park, where you'll find another four miles' worth of loops. After you finish the first five miles along the river, things get more interesting. Your ride through the residential neighborhoods will give you a taste of the hills you can expect when you get to Detweiller Park. The ride up Grandview Drive, for instance, features a rough hill with a view of the surrounding area. This is a fashionable neighborhood, so feel free to admire the homes. In fact, you'll be near an older historic area with many quaint shops.

By the time you get to Detweiller Park, the trail picks up again and the real mountain biking begins. In Detweiller, there are actually three trails from which to choose: Pimiteoui, Ridge Top, and Dry Run. These loop trails are quite demanding because of their narrower single-track. You'll also have to contend with many obstacles in the dense woods—such as fallen trees—on these unmaintained trails. Of course, what will really get you are the hills. The climbs will be challenging by central Illinois standards, but the view of the Illinois River will be worth it. At the water crossings, be prepared to ride over logs. Since the area borders a major city, you won't find a lot of wildlife, but you'll want to come here for the scenery and the hills. Also, for you BMX riders, there's a BMX course next to Detweiller Park.

General location: On the east side of Peoria.
Elevation change: You'll find an elevation gain of roughly 300 feet.
Season: You can ride this trail all year. Because of the tree cover, the trail doesn't get very muddy. In the fall, the Illinois River Valley is one of the prettiest areas in the state.
Services: Detweiller Park has water. All services are available in Peoria. If you need help with your bike, visit Russell's Cycle World in Washington.
Hazards: Look out for the obstacles on the single-track—expect to dismount.
Rescue index: Shelters are located throughout the park, so you're never more than 5 or 10 minutes from a phone. You'll find light traffic on the roads.
Land status: Peoria Park District.
Maps: The USGS 7.5 minute quads are Peoria East and Spring Bay.
Finding the trail: From downtown Peoria, take Interstate 74 south and get off at the Adams exit. Go west on Adams for a couple of blocks to Hamilton. Turn left on Hamilton and take that a short way down to the river. Park by the metered parking by the Boat Works.

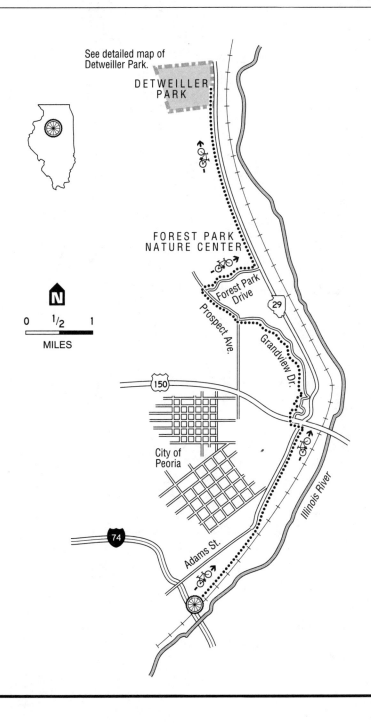

See detailed map of
Detweiller Park.

DETWEILLER
PARK

FOREST PARK
NATURE CENTER

Forest Park
Drive

Prospect Ave.

Grandview Dr.

29

N

0   1/2   1
MILES

150

City of
Peoria

Illinois River

74

Adams St.

RIDE 50 *PIMITEOUI TRAIL / DETWEILLER PARK*

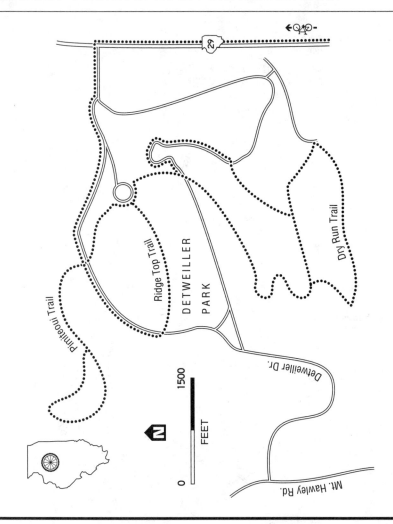

Sources of additional information:

Peoria Park District
Glen Oak Pavillion
2218 North Prospect Road
Peoria, IL 61603
(309) 682-1200

Russell's Cycle World
308 North Main
Washington, IL 61571
(309) 444-2098

Notes on the trail: The ride begins directly underneath I-74. Follow the trail for 5 miles until you get to US 150. At the war memorial, take US 150 about 3 miles to Grandview Drive. Enjoy the hill and the view, and take Grandview to Prospect Avenue. When you get to Prospect Avenue, take a right and go about 1 mile to Forest Park Drive. Turn right on Forest Park Drive. (If you go left on Forest Park Drive, you'll hit the shops in the historic area.) You'll pass the Forest Park Nature Center, where you can stop for a visit if you like on these restricted trails. Forest Park Drive connects with Galena Road (IL 29). Take Galena Road 3 miles into Detweiller Park, where you can pick up the trail.

There is conflicting information as to whether or not Detweiller Park is accessible to mountain bikes. Call to confirm its availability before you ride.

RIDE 51 *FARMDALE RECREATION AREA*

You can do two kinds of rides at Farmdale Recreation Area. For those of you looking for an easy ride, follow the dirt roads that cross through the low-lying areas. The roads make for good family riding. But for those of you looking for more adventure, turn onto any of the dirt trails you find branching off the roads. These trails will be narrower, more difficult to climb, and fraught with several challenging obstacles—not the least of which will be planning your own loops and out-and-backs from the maps available. There are simply too many trails for me to direct you to any *one* of them without confusion.

Between the easy and more difficult riding in Farmdale, you'll have about ten miles of trails to ride. Even the easier sections aren't without their taunts, as you'll encounter three major creek crossings. Plan to get your feet wet! On the more difficult spurs, the grade will test your climbing ability. It will be well worth it when you find a nice, smooth trail waiting for you at the summit. You'll also have to skirt around rocks, branches, and smaller, yet more difficult, stream crossings than the ones on the easier route. Deer and coyote can also be found in this wooded area. In essence, Farmdale Recreation Area has a variety of terrains and levels of difficulty—something for everyone.

General location: In East Peoria, ten minutes from Peoria.
Elevation change: The elevation gain is roughly 100 feet.
Season: Summer, fall, and winter are best. Avoid the spring, when it can get quite wet.

RIDE 51 *FARMDALE RECREATION AREA*

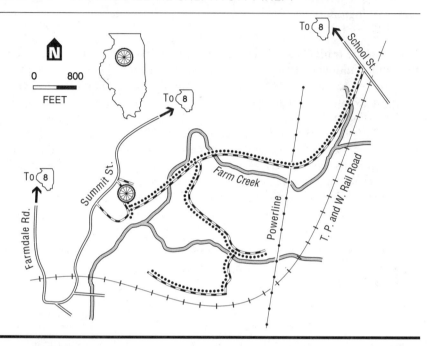

Services: There is a campground in Farmdale Recreation Area. Food and lodging are available in East Peoria. All services are available in Peoria. Russell's Cycle World in Washington offers bicycle service.

Hazards: Be careful at the water crossings. In the more demanding areas, the obstacles can present some difficulties.

Rescue index: From anywhere in Farmdale, you're only minutes from a road where you can flag down help.

Land status: U.S. Army Corps of Engineers—Rock Island District.

Maps: The Army Corps of Engineers has a map listing the easier route without the spurs. Write for one at the address below. The USGS 7.5 minute quads for this area are Washington and Peoria East.

Finding the trail: Take Interstate 74 south out of Peoria to IL 8. Take IL 8 east about 3 miles to Farmdale Road and turn right. Go 2 miles to Summit Street. Turn left on Summit Street and follow it a short way to the parking area.

Sources of additional information:

Park Ranger
U.S. Army Corps of Engineers
Foot of Grant Street

Peoria, IL 61603
(309) 676-4601

Russell's Cycle World
308 North Main
Washington, IL 61571
(309) 444-2098

Notes on the trail: Pick up the trail from the parking lot. It's a dirt road that travels throughout the park. The map included in this guide lists only the easier, dirt-road ride; the more challenging spurs are not shown.

RIDE 52 McNAUGHTON PARK

Looking for a little challenge? You'll find both easy and difficult trail riding at McNaughton Park, but for the most part, this area can be challenging. McNaughton Park consists of two connecting loops—the Potawatomi Trail and the Running Deer Trail—for a total distance of about 12 miles. Primarily, both trails are wide, ranging from one to four bike widths. Potawatomi is wider than Running Deer, and its dirt trail gets a little sandier as you approach the creeks. You'll find many steep, short climbs and creek crossings, making this a moderate to challenging ride. Running Deer Trail is also dirt but has a few more grassy sections than Potawatomi. The difficulty of this trail ranges from easy to challenging, and you'll find a few sections where the trail has narrow uphills and white-knuckle descents. It's easy to slip on these narrow hills, so no one will think less of you if you decide to walk your bike down. There are more roots and obstacles on Running Deer Trail than on the other, and it has creek crossings to test your "wetness quotient."

Those who want their wooded trails to give them the same emotional ups and downs as the terrain will like McNaughton Park. You'll appreciate the nice, rolling, smooth sections as well as the technical, endurance-testing ones.

General location: Just east of Pekin.
Elevation change: The elevation changes range around 100 feet.
Season: Plan on riding here in the summer and the winter when the trails are drier than the spring.
Services: Water is available at the trailhead. Pekin has all services. For bike service, visit Russell's Cycle World in Washington.
Hazards: The water crossings, and some of the narrower passages on the hills, can be hazardous.
Rescue index: You're never far from a road where you can flag down help.

RIDE 52 *McNAUGHTON PARK*

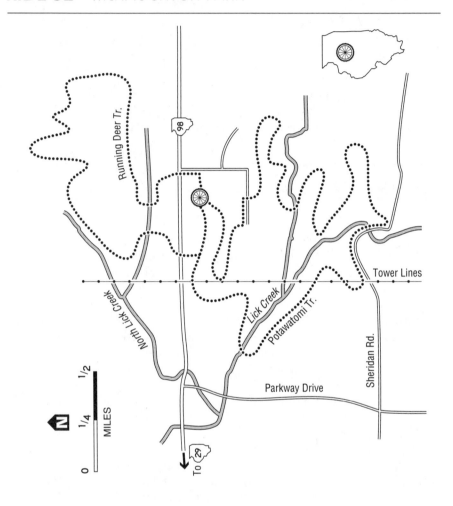

Land status: Pekin Park District.

Maps: You can write the Pekin Park District at the address below for a map of the park. The USGS 7.5 minute quad for this area is Marquette Heights.

Finding the trail: Take IL 29 out of Peoria; when you get to Pekin, take IL 98 east (left). Go approximately 4 miles on IL 98 and you'll see the park on the right side of the road.

Sources of additional information:

Pekin Park District
1701 Court Street
Pekin, IL 61554
(309) 34R-PARK

Russell's Cycle World
308 North Main
Washington, IL 61571
(309) 444-2098

Notes on the trail: You'll see 3 trailheads from the parking area. Take whichever trail you desire because they all loop back to the start. The trails aren't marked, but can be followed easily. The intersection of the 2 trails isn't marked, but it's also easy to find.

East Central Illinois

East central Illinois is not the mountain bike capital of the world, but that doesn't mean you can't dig up a few high-quality rides in the area. For instance, as you ride down Interstate 74, it's all corn, but suddenly you come to a heavily forested area and you wonder, is this a good spot for mountain biking? The spot is Kickapoo State Park and the answer is a resounding "Yes." You'll even find some sheer drop-offs and hill climbing to test both your endurance and your technical skills. Says Fritz Miericke of Champaign Cycle, "It's a good place to go to if you like to go off-road and not be surrounded by corn and beans."

Further south, you'll find the Chief Illini Trail and Newton Lake. The Chief Illini Trail is also surprisingly challenging for its location in the state. As you look down the ravines on this ride, you'll wonder where the corn is. Newton Lake is not as difficult as the other two, but it will provide a nice getaway ride in a not too densely populated part of the state.

Thanks to Fritz Miericke for information about Kickapoo State Park and Derrick Moscardelli for information about the Chief Illini Trail.

RIDE 53 *KICKAPOO STATE PARK*

With most state parks, it's up to the site manager to determine whether mountain biking will be permitted. Kickapoo State Park is the first to get official approval through the Illinois Department of Conservation—and the mountain bikers of east central Illinois are grateful! In an area where you wouldn't expect to find mountain bike opportunities, there's an area of 1,500 acres set aside for mountain bike use. Currently five and a half miles of beginning trails cut their way in three loops through a reclaimed strip mine area where tractors first plowed an eight-foot-wide path. Then the trail was cleared of stumps and other debris. As this guide goes to press, plans are underway to develop another 25 to 30 miles of intermediate and expert trails. At one time, this area was set aside for motorcycle use, but the trails have since been abandoned. Members of the Kickapoo Mountain Bike Club are in the process of "rediscovering" them.

"This is as close as we get to hills and rough stuff," says Fritz Miericke, a member of the Kickapoo Bike Club. And Fritz is right. You'll find moderate climbs, some of which can be technically challenging, that weave in and out of ridges and around creeks. At the top of one of the major ridges, you'll get a great view of the tree line below. At the bottom, you'll find a nice, quiet pond. In fact, you'll encounter several ponds in the area. For those who want to get their feet

RIDE 53 *KICKAPOO STATE PARK*

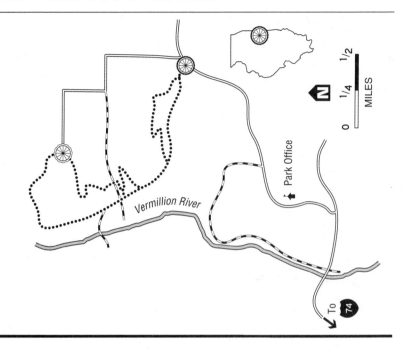

wet, there are several water crossings. Kickapoo is not without its difficulties. As you ride through the trees, you'll need to pay attention to the direction of the trail, as there are some sheer drop-offs. Also, keep your eyes peeled for deer and eagles. Kickapoo State Park, with its five and a half miles currently developed, is a great place to ride. When the rest is finished, you'll find a mountain bike oasis in the middle of corn country.

General location: Kickapoo State Park is in Oakwood, 10 miles west of Danville.

Elevation change: The elevation change ranges around 50 feet.

Season: The fall and early spring are best because it's drier, and you'll be able to see the landscape changes more easily. In the summer, you'll have to contend with heat and deerflies.

Services: Kickapoo State Park has camping, fishing, boating, and canoe rentals. All services are available in either Danville or Champaign-Urbana. I recommend Champaign Cycle in Champaign for bicycle service.

Hazards: You'll need to pay attention and look ahead where the trail dips down to avoid those cliffs.

Rescue index: You can get assistance from the ranger station at the park entrance.

Land status: State park.

Maps: The USGS 7.5 minute quads for Kickapoo State Park are Danville NW and Collison.

Finding the trail: Follow Interstate 74 west out of Danville about 10 miles and take the Oakwood exit. Go north 3.5 miles and follow the signs to Kickapoo State Park. Stop at the ranger station for directions to the trailhead.

Sources of additional information:

> Kickapoo State Park
> 10906 Kickapoo Park Road
> Oakwood, IL 61858
> (217) 442-4915

> Champaign Cycle
> 506 South Country Fair Drive
> Champaign, IL 61821
> (217) 352-7600

> Kickapoo Mountain Bike Club
> 506 South Country Fair Drive
> Champaign, IL 61821

Notes on the trail: The 5.5 miles of loop trails are well marked. As the other trails are developed, they will also be marked. Make sure you stay on the mountain bike trails and keep off the horse trails and walking paths.

RIDE 54 *CHIEF ILLINI TRAIL*

The Chief Illini Trail runs along the edge of Lake Shelbyville, a popular boating and camping area in Illinois. And after riding this trail, you'll need to unwind out on the lake. While this out-and-back dirt trail is 11 miles one-way (22 miles total), at this point only the lower 4 miles are open to cyclists. That's because the Army Corps of Engineers controls those four; the rest are controlled by the state. Perhaps someday the rest will become available. But don't let the limited distance of this ride deter you; you'll find enough to challenge both your riding skills and your endurance. You know you will be tested from the beginning of this trail as you walk your bike down a series of stairs. The trail is well maintained, but narrow—often only a couple of feet wide, cut into the side of a hill. If you lose your concentration, you could go tumbling down the ravine.

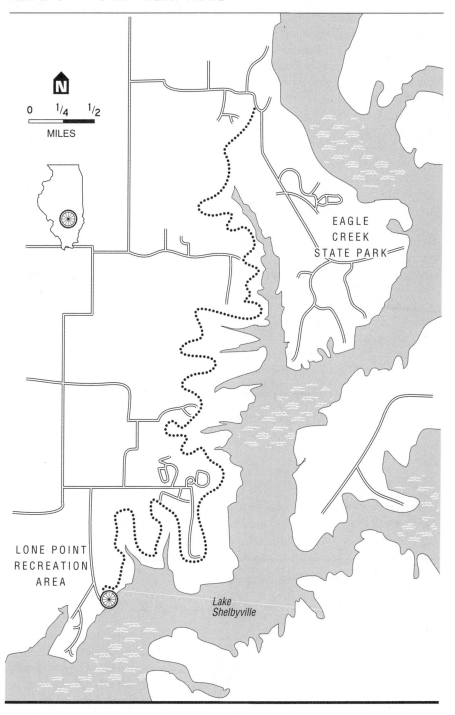

MILES

EAGLE
CREEK
STATE PARK

LONE POINT
RECREATION
AREA

*Lake
Shelbyville*

That's the technical part. The test of endurance comes when the trail hits the bottom of a ravine and you have a straight shot back up with no momentum. Be prepared to walk your bike. Even a creek crossing can be a harbinger of impending stamina requirements. As you come out of a water crossing, you'll be faced with another steep climb. The trail is scenic, though. You'll enjoy the Midwestern forest (with a few fields here and there) and the occasional views of the lake itself.

General location: Thirty-one miles southeast of Decatur.

Elevation change: While the climbs are steep, the overall elevation change is less than 100 feet.

Season: The fall is scenic, and when the leaves are down you'll get better views of Lake Shelbyville. In the summer watch out for poison ivy.

Services: Water is available at the trailhead. Camping is available at Lake Shelbyville. There is a bike shop in the city of Shelbyville.

Hazards: The narrowness of the trail along the ravine is your most challenging hazard.

Rescue index: At several points along the trail, you pass over or near some roads. You'll usually find visitors at the Lone Point Recreation Area trailhead.

Land status: U.S. Army Corps of Engineers.

Maps: The U.S. Army Corps of Engineers has a fine map available at the address below. The USGS 7.5 minute quad for this area is Middlesworth.

Finding the trail: Take IL 128 south out of Findlay and follow the signs for 5 miles to the trailhead at Lone Point Recreation Area.

Sources of additional information:

Lake Shelbyville Management Office
U.S. Army Corps of Engineers
RR 4, Box 128 B
Shelbyville, IL 62565
(217) 774-3951

Notes on the trail: The trailhead is signed at the southwest corner of the parking lot, the trail is marked with white blazes and mile markers.

RIDE 55 _NEWTON LAKE_

Newton Lake has chickens—not just any old chickens, but rare prairie chickens. You won't actually see them from the trail on the west side of the lake, but they are there on the east side. Ridden one way, the trail goes out a distance of 12 miles (24 miles total). On the return, you can follow the same route back or

RIDE 55 *NEWTON LAKE*

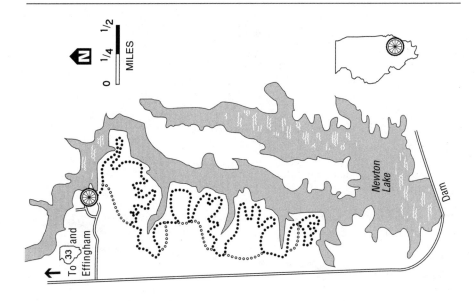

take one of several shortcut loops back to the trailhead. Half of the dirt horse trail passes through the woods and the other half goes through grass fields. The trail is wide, easy to follow, and well maintained, so people of all abilities should be able to enjoy it. However, it can be rough from equestrian use. There aren't a lot of big hills, but you'll encounter a few sharp curves. Also, you'll enjoy quite a few gravelly creek crossings. Along the way, stop at the rest areas for a scenic view of the lake. You may not see any chickens, but perhaps you'll spot a pair of bald eagles.

General location: About 20 miles southeast of Effingham.
Elevation change: You'll pass in and out of hills, but any gain is insignificant.
Season: Summer is the best time to ride because it's drier. The trails may be closed when wet, especially in the winter and early spring, so check ahead at the address listed below.
Services: Water is available at the office. Food and lodging can be found in Newton. For bicycle service, go to Effingham.
Hazards: Some caution is needed going through the creek beds. Look out for hikers and horses.

Rescue index: There is a phone at the office. You should see other trail users or boaters out on the lake.

Land status: Illinois Department of Conservation.

Maps: Newton Lake has a good map showing the trail and the various short-cut options. Write for it at the address below. The USGS 7.5 minute quad for this area is Latona.

Finding the trail: From Effingham, take IL 33 south about 20 miles. The signs will direct you to Newton Lake. Park at the North Access.

Sources of additional information:

> Newton Lake State Fish and Wildlife Area
> RR 4
> Box 178B
> Newton, IL 62448
> (618) 783-3478

Notes on the trail: From the North Access, you'll see the sign for the trailhead. The trail is marked, especially the points which show the trail shortcuts.

Shawnee National Forest

I grew up in the northern part of the state, so southern Illinois was as foreign to me as Burma or Cameroon. When I first talked to folks about Shawnee National Forest, I asked, "Hey, you guys have rattlesnakes down there, don't you?" The response was, "It's not the rattlesnakes you need to worry about; it's the copperheads." And when I saw a copperhead on one of the trails—albeit dead—I realized I wasn't in my backyard anymore.

Poisonous snakes aside, Shawnee National Forest has a few good places to ride. Admittedly, the policies at this forest are more restrictive than Hoosier National Forest in Indiana or Wayne National Forest in Ohio, but what is available will provide some exciting, if not physically challenging, riding.

The eastern districts of Shawnee National Forest attract more tourists, especially in the Garden of the Gods area, but the rides I've included are in the western side of the forest, where you'll find fewer people. Cedar Lake and Kinkaid Lake Trails will give you a chance to test your technical abilities and your endurance. The Pine Hills Ride, while not technically difficult, will remind you that southern Illinois is not flat. You'll climb your way up the hills and see spectacular vistas below.

RIDE 56 *KINKAID LAKE—BUTTERMILK HILL*

This roughly 15-mile one-way (30 mile total) out-and-back features some aggressive dirt single-track, but also overlooks beautiful Kinkaid Lake. As you begin the ride near Crisenberry Dam, you will immediately encounter many roots and rocks, and all but the best riders will probably portage the beginning. But take heart—it does get better. The obstacle-rich trail becomes easier to ride, allowing you the opportunity to glimpse the shoreline and boating on the lake. You'll ride along the slopes above the lake through a diverse section of timber. Expect the trail to become very rocky again just past Buttermilk Hill Beach and just before Hidden Cove. Your stamina will be tested mostly as you navigate through the rocky sections. If you're quiet, perhaps you'll glimpse wild turkey and deer. If you're too tired to make the return ride, try renting a boat at the Johnson Creek Recreation Area at the other trailhead.

General location: Shawnee National Forest, 7.5 miles west of Murphysboro.
Elevation change: The overall elevation gain amounts to around 100 feet. There are no really steep climbs. The steepest section is by the dam.

RIDE 56 *KINKAID LAKE / BUTTERMILK HILL*

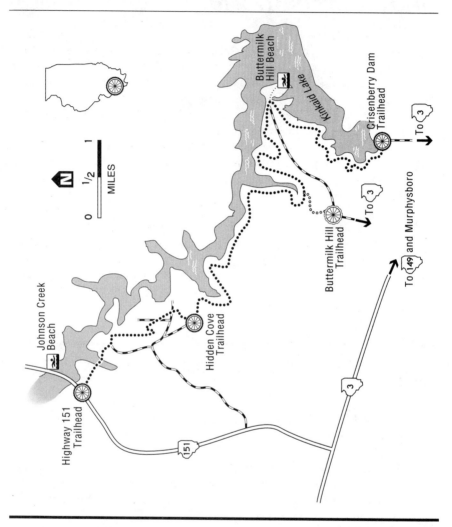

Season: Early spring and early fall are best because the temperatures are more temperate than other times of year. The fall colors around the lake make for a picture-perfect panorama.

Services: There is no water at the State trailhead (Crisenberry Dam), but the Highway 151 trailhead by Johnson Creek Recreation Area has water. Food and lodging are available in Murphysboro. For bicycle service, consider Phoenix Cycles in Carbondale.

The technical single-track will attract the expert rider.

Hazards: Aside from the slippery sections near the rocky portions, there are rattlesnakes and copperheads in this area.

Rescue index: There is a phone at Johnson Creek Recreation Area. If you get into trouble, you can make your way down to the lake to flag down a boater.

Land status: Shawnee National Forest—Murphysboro Ranger District.

Maps: You can get a map of the trail from Shawnee National Forest. Write to the address below. The USGS 7.5 minute quad for Lake Kinkaid is Oraville, and the IL 151 trailhead spills onto the Raddle quad.

Finding the trail: To the Dam (State) trailhead: From IL 127 in Murphysboro, take IL 149 west for 7.3 miles to Spillway Road and turn right. (Note: Don't turn where you see a sign for Kinkaid Lake.) Go 1.7 miles to the parking area. To get to the trailhead, ride back to the parking area entrance and turn right. Go up the gravel road. The trail entrance will be on your left, marked by some wooden beams.

To the Buttermilk Hill trailhead: From IL 127 in Murphysboro, take IL 149 west for 8 miles. Turn right on IL 3 and go 1.5 miles to a sign for the Buttermilk Hill trailhead. Turn right and follow the signs to the parking area. To get to the trailhead from the parking area, ride down the short grassy trail until you see the trail markers.

To the Highway 151 trailhead: From IL 127 in Murphysboro, take IL 149 west for 8 miles. Turn right on IL 3 and go 4.5 miles to IL 151. Turn right. Just before you get to Johnson Creek Road, about 5 miles, look carefully to your right for a sign for the Route 151 trailhead. For parking, keep heading down toward the Johnson Creek Recreation Area.

Sources of additional information:

> U.S. Forest Service
> Murphysboro Ranger District
> 2221 Walnut, P.O. Box 787
> Murphysboro, IL 62966-0787
> (618) 687-1731

> Phoenix Cycles
> 300 South Illinois Avenue
> Carbondale, IL 62901
> (618) 549-3612

Notes on the trail: While finding the trailhead off Spillway Road can be tricky, the trail itself is well marked by white diamonds. As you ride the trail, of course, don't feel obligated to ride the branch down to the Buttermilk Hill trailhead. Head toward the Hidden Cove trailhead if you wish.

RIDE 57 *CEDAR LAKE TRAIL*

You'll get a little workout riding the rolling hills on this trail. The 11-mile (total distance) out-and-back portion of this ride travels along the west side of Cedar Lake before making a four-mile loop around Little Cedar Lake. (Your out-and-back and loop trail total is therefore 15 miles.) The fun on the loop portion begins right away with a series of moguls before the trail crosses over the rocky foundation separating the two lakes. Most of the trail is dirt single-track and easily passable, but there are some rocky stretches just north of Pomona Road requiring technical skills. You may need to get off and portage. Most of the trail won't require as many technical skills as this section, but you'll need energy for climbing the short hills. Don't worry—there's nothing too steep.

Most of the trail travels through the forest surrounding the lake, and several spots on the out-and-back section offer gorgeous views of the lake. Near Cove Hollow, you'll find a unique feature: several rock shelters where you can stop and rest. While not quite caves, these natural formations are large enough to enter. You won't need your spelunking gear.

General location: Shawnee National Forest, 10 miles south of Murphysboro.
Elevation change: You'll experience about 100 feet of elevation change.

RIDE 57 *CEDAR LAKE TRAIL*

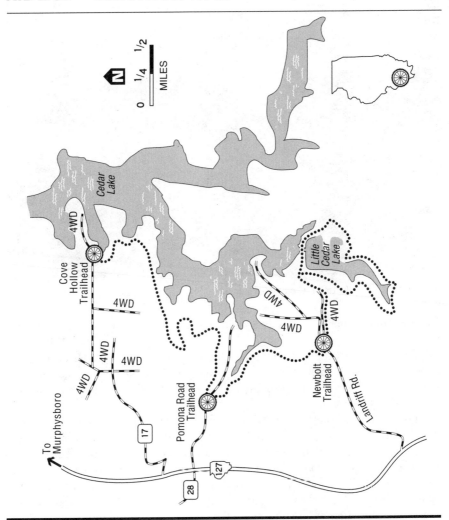

Season: The best riding is in the early spring and early fall. Ticks and heat can be a problem during the summer months.

Services: Bring your own water. Food and lodging are available in Murphysboro. For bicycle service, visit Phoenix Cycles in Carbondale.

Hazards: Use a little caution on the rockier section of the trail. Rattlesnakes and copperheads can be found here. When I visited, I saw a dead copperhead in the middle of the trail.

Look out at Little Cedar Lake from the trail.

Rescue index: The lake often has boaters and fishermen. There are also some residences in the area.

Land status: Shawnee National Forest—Murphysboro Ranger District.

Maps: Shawnee National Forest has a map with topographical markings of Cedar Lake. Write to the address below. The USGS 7.5 minute quads are Pomona and Cobden.

Finding the trail: To Newbolt trailhead: From the intersection of IL 149 and IL 127 in Murphysboro, go south on Route 127 about 20 miles to Landriff Road, which is at the dividing line between Jackson and Union Counties. Turn left on Landriff. The gravel road will end soon and turn to double-track. Since your vehicles may have difficulty traveling down the double-track, you might wish to park off the side of the road and ride the mile or so to the trailhead marker.

Contact the Murphysboro Ranger District for directions to the Cove Hollow and Pomona Road trailheads.

Sources of additional information:

U.S. Forest Service
Murphysboro Ranger District
2221 Walnut, P.O. Box 787
Murphysboro, IL 62966-0787
(618) 687-1731

Phoenix Cycles
300 South Illinois Avenue
Carbondale, IL 62901
(618) 549-3612

Notes on the trail: Beginning at the Newbolt trailhead will give you the option of doing just the 4-mile loop around Little Cedar Lake or heading north on the out-and-back to Cove Hollow. To enter the loop trail, follow the narrow grass single-track from the trailhead marker. After you cross over to the east side of Little Cedar Lake, turn right and follow the trail around.

RIDE 58 *PINE HILLS RIDE*

Are you looking for a non-technical ride that challenges your stamina, yet affords some of the most spectacular views in Illinois? If so, this ride is for you. This 16-mile loop skirts the western border of the Clear Springs Wilderness Area in Shawnee National Forest. The first 11 miles of the loop are on gravel and dirt Forest Service roads, but to complete the loop, you'll travel the last 5 miles on a paved state highway.

As you travel down the heavily forested area around Forest Service Road 236, several scenic vistas await you. From the Crooked Tree Observation Area, you'll be able to see the Missouri Ridge Line in the distance. You might want to get off your bike and take a short hiking trail down for a secluded view. Other impressive views await you at Saddle Hill, Pine Ridge, and Old Trail Point. The gravel road is not technically challenging, but it will require a modest amount of exertion because of the 300-foot elevation gain. All this changes drastically, though, once you hit Forest Service Road 345. You now leave the forest and head down a flat, dirt road along the wetlands. Winters Pond is an old borrow pit, an area where soil was "borrowed" to build up a nearby levee. Over time, water and plants filled in the pit, creating the wetlands.

General location: Shawnee National Forest, 21 miles northwest of the intersection of Interstate 57 and IL 146, near the town of Wolf Lake.
Elevation change: The ride begins at 420 feet and gains 300 feet. The stretch down FS 345 is virtually flat.
Season: This ride is the southernmost ride in the book. A southern Illinois summer can be quite hot. Nevertheless, I like the summer green on this ride. Of course, autumn views at the vistas are quite remarkable, too.
Services: Primitive camping and water are available at the Pine Hills Campground. Food and lodging are available in Anna. For bicycle repair, try Phoenix Cycles in Carbondale.

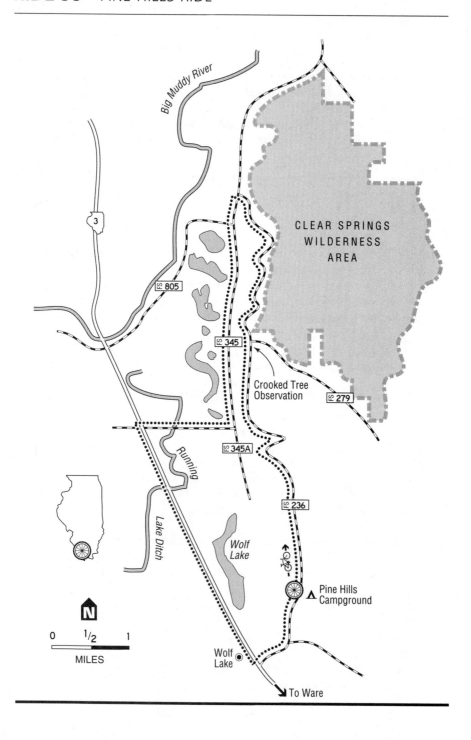

Big Muddy River

3

CLEAR SPRINGS
WILDERNESS
AREA

FS 805

FS 345

Crooked Tree
Observation

FS 279

FS 345A

Running

FS 236

Lake Ditch

Wolf
Lake

Pine Hills
Campground

N

0   1/2   1
MILES

Wolf
Lake

To Ware

The serenity of Shawnee National Forest makes for a secluded ride just miles from the Missouri border.

Hazards: You'll find no obstacles to speak of here, but the traffic on IL 3 can be swift.

Rescue index: Forest Service Road 236 and FS 345 have light traffic, and IL 3 has much more.

Land status: Shawnee National Forest.

Maps: The USGS 7.5 minute quad is Wolf Lake.

Finding the trail: From I-57, take Exit 30, IL 146 for Anna/Vienna. Go right (west) on IL 146 for 15.5 miles. At IL 3 in Ware, turn right (north) for 4 miles. When you get near the town of Wolf Lake, look for an unmarked road with the sign, "Trail of Tears State Forest—Indian State Nursery." Turn right on that road, and shortly, you'll come to FS 236. Turn left and go to the Larue-Pine Hills Campground. You can begin your ride here.

Sources of additional information:

Shawnee National Forest
901 South Commercial Street
Harrisburg, IL 62946
(618) 253-7114

Notes on the trail: From the LaRue-Pine Hills Campground, turn right, heading north on FS 236. After 7 miles, turn left on FS 345 (Pine Hills Road). Four and a half miles later, you'll hit IL 3. Turn left and go 3.5 miles to the road marked "Trail of Tears State Forest." Turn left again and go back to FS 236. Turn left and head to the campground.

Stay out of the Wilderness Area.

Afterword

LAND-USE CONTROVERSY

A few years ago I wrote a long piece on this issue for *Sierra* magazine that entailed calling literally dozens of government land managers, game wardens, mountain bikers, and local officials to get a feeling for how riders were being welcomed on the trails. All that I've seen personally since, and heard from my authors, indicates there hasn't been much change. We're still considered the new kid on the block. We have less of a right to the trails than equestrians and hikers, and we're excluded from many areas, including:

a) wilderness areas

b) national parks (except on roads, and those paths specifically marked "bike path")

c) national monuments (except on roads open to the public)

d) most state parks and monuments (except on roads, and those paths specifically marked "bike path")

e) an increasing number of urban and county parks, especially in California (except on roads, and those paths specifically marked "bike path")

Frankly, I have little difficulty with these exclusions and would, in fact, restrict our presence from some trails I've ridden (one time) due to the environmental damage and chance of blindsiding the many walkers and hikers I met up with along the way. But these are my personal views. The author of this volume and mountain bikers as a group may hold different opinions.

You can do your part in keeping us from being excluded from even more trails by riding responsibly. Many local and national off-road bicycle organizations have been formed with exactly this in mind, and one of the largest—the National Off-Road Bicycle Association (NORBA)—offers the following code of behavior for mountain bikers:

1. I will yield the right of way to other non-motorized recreationists. I realize that people judge all cyclists by my actions.

2. I will slow down and use caution when approaching or overtaking another cyclist and will make my presence known well in advance.

3. I will maintain control of my speed at all times and will approach turns in anticipation of someone around the bend.

4. I will stay on designated trails to avoid trampling native vegetation and minimize potential erosion to trails by not using muddy trails or short-cutting switchbacks.

5. I will not disturb wildlife or livestock.

6. I will not litter. I will pack out what I pack in, and pack out more than my share whenever possible.

7. I will respect public and private property, including trail use signs and no trespassing signs, and I will leave gates as I have found them.

8. I will always be self-sufficient and my destination and travel speed will be determined by my ability, my equipment, the terrain, the present and potential weather conditions.

9. I will not travel solo when bikepacking in remote areas. I will leave word of my destination and when I plan to return.

10. I will observe the practice of minimum impact bicycling by "taking only pictures and memories and leaving only waffle prints."

11. I will always wear a helmet whenever I ride.

Now, I have a problem with some of these—number nine, for instance. The most enjoyable mountain biking I've ever done has been solo. And as for leaving word of destination and time of return, I've enjoyed living in such a way as to say, "I'm off to pedal Colorado. See you in the fall." Of course it's senseless to take needless risks, and I plan a ride and pack my gear with this in mind. But for me number nine smacks too much of the "never-out-of-touch" mentality. And getting away from civilization, deep into the wild, is, for many people, what mountain biking's all about.

All in all, however, NORBA's is a good list, and surely we mountain bikers would be liked more, and excluded less, if we followed the suggestions. But let me offer a "code of ethics" I much prefer, one given to cyclists by Utah's Wasatch-Cache National Forest office.

Study a Forest Map Before You Ride

Currently, bicycles are permitted on roads and developed trails within the Wasatch-Cache National Forest except in designated Wilderness. If your route crosses private land, it is your responsibility to obtain right of way permission from the landowner.

Keep Groups Small

Riding in large groups degrades the outdoor experience for others, can disturb wildlife, and usually leads to greater resource damage.

Avoid Riding on Wet Trails
Bicycle tires leave ruts in wet trails. These ruts concentrate runoff and accelerate erosion. Postponing a ride when the trails are wet will reserve the trails for future use.

Stay on Roads and Trails
Riding cross-country destroys vegetation and damages the soil.

Always Yield to Others
Trails are shared by hikers, horses, and bicycles. Move off the trail to allow horses to pass and stop to allow hikers adequate room to share the trail. Simply yelling "Bicycle!" is not acceptable.

Control Your Speed
Excessive speed endangers yourself and other forest users.

Avoid Wheel Lock-up and Spin-out
Steep terrain is especially vulnerable to trail wear. Locking brakes on steep descents or when stopping needlessly damages trails. If a slope is steep enough to require locking wheels and skidding, dismount and walk your bicycle. Likewise, if an ascent is so steep your rear wheel slips and spins, dismount and walk your bicycle.

Protect Waterbars and Switchbacks
Waterbars, the rock and log drains built to direct water off trails, protect trails from erosion. When you encounter a waterbar, ride directly over the top or dismount and walk your bicycle. Riding around the ends of water-bars destroys them and speeds erosion. Skidding around switchback corners shortens trail life. Slow down for switchback corners and keep your wheels rolling.

If You Abuse It, You Lose It
Mountain bikers are relative newcomers to the forest and must prove themselves responsible trail users. By following the guidelines above, and by participating in trail maintenance service projects, bicyclists can help avoid closures which would prevent them from using trails.

I've never seen a better trail-etiquette list for mountain bikers. So have fun. Be careful. And don't screw things up for the next rider.

Dennis Coello
Series Editor

Glossary

This short list of terms does not contain all the words used by mountain bike enthusiasts when discussing their sport. But it should serve as an introduction to the lingo you'll hear on the trails.

ATB
all-terrain bike; this, like "fat-tire bike," is another name for a mountain bike

ATV
all-terrain vehicle; this usually refers to the loud, fume-spewing three- or four-wheeled motorized vehicles you will not enjoy meeting on the trail—except, of course, if you crash and have to hitch a ride out on one

bladed
refers to a dirt road that has been smoothed out by the use of a wide blade on earth-moving equipment; "blading" gets rid of the teeth-chattering, much-cursed washboards found on so many dirt roads after heavy vehicle use

blaze
a mark on a tree made by chipping away a piece of the bark, usually done to designate a trail; such trails are sometimes described as "blazed"

blind corner
a curve in a road or trail that conceals bikers, hikers, equestrians and other traffic

BLM
Bureau of Land Management, an agency of the federal government

buffed
used to describe a very smooth trail

catching air
taking a jump in such a way that both wheels of the bike are off the ground at the same time

clean
while this may describe what you and your bike won't be after following many trials, the term is most often used as a verb to denote the action of pedaling a tough section of trail successfully

combination
this type of route may combine two or more configurations; for example, a point-to-point route may integrate a scenic loop or out-and-back spur midway through the ride; likewise, an out-and-back may have a loop at its farthest point (this configuration looks like a cherry with stem attached; the stem is the out-and-back, the fruit is the terminus loop); or a loop route may have multiple out-

and-back spurs and/or loops to the side; mileage for a combination route is for the total distance to complete the ride

dab   touching the ground with a foot or hand

deadfall   a tangled mass of fallen trees or branches

diversion ditch   a usually narrow, shallow ditch dug across or around a trail; funneling the water in this manner keeps it from destroying the trail

double-track   the dual tracks made by a jeep or other vehicle, with grass or weeds or rocks between; mountain bikers can ride in either of the tracks, but you will of course find that whichever one you choose, and no matter how many times you change back and forth, the other track will appear to offer smoother travel

dugway   a steep, unpaved, switchbacked descent

endo   flipping end over end

feathering   using a light touch on the brake lever, hitting it lightly many times rather than very hard or locking the brake

four-wheel-drive   this refers to any vehicle with drive-wheel capability on all four wheels (a jeep, for instance, has four-wheel drive as compared with a two-wheel-drive passenger car), or to a rough road or trail that requires four-wheel-drive capability (or a one-wheel-drive mountain bike!) to negotiate it

game trail   the usually narrow trail made by deer, elk, or other game

gated   everyone knows what a gate is, and how many variations exist upon this theme; well, if a trail is described as "gated" it simply has a gate across it; don't forget that the rule is if you find a gate closed, close it behind you; if you find one open, leave it that way

Giardia   shorthand for *Giardia lamblia*, and known as the "backpacker's bane" until we mountain bikers expropriated it; this is a waterborne parasite that begins its life cycle when swallowed, and one to four weeks later has its host (you) bloated, vomiting, shivering with chills and living in the bathroom; the disease can be avoided by "treating" (purifying) the water you acquire along the trail (see "Hitting the Trail" in the Introduction)

gnarly   a term thankfully used less and less these days, it refers to tough trails

hammer	to ride very hard
hardpack	a trail in which the dirt surface is packed down hard; such trails make for good and fast riding, and very painful landings; bikers most often use "hardpack" as both noun and adjective, and "hardpacked" as an adjective only (the grammar lesson will help you when diagramming sentences in camp)
hike-a-bike	what you do when the road or trail becomes too steep or rough to remain in the saddle
jeep road, jeep trail	a rough road or trail passable only with four-wheel-drive capability (or a horse or mountain bike)
kamikaze	while this once referred primarily to those Japanese fliers who quaffed a glass of saké, then flew off as human bombs in suicide missions against U.S. naval vessels, it has more recently been applied to the idiot mountain bikers who, far less honorably, scream down hiking trails, endangering the physical and mental safety of the walking, biking, and equestrian traffic they meet; deck guns were necessary to stop the Japanese kamikaze pilots, but a bike pump or walking staff in the spokes is sufficient for the current-day kamikazes who threaten to get us all kicked off the trails
loop	this route configuration is characterized by riding from the designated trailhead to a distant point, then returning to the trailhead via a different route (or simply continuing on the same in a circle route) without doubling back; you always move forward across new terrain, but return to the starting point when finished; mileage is for the entire loop from the trailhead back to trailhead
multi-purpose	a BLM designation of land which is open to many uses; mountain biking is allowed
ORV	a motorized off-road vehicle
out-and-back	a ride where you will return on the same trail on which you pedaled out; while this might sound far more boring than a loop route, many trails look very different when pedaled in the opposite direction; unless otherwise noted, mileage figures are the *total* distance out *and* back.
pack stock	horses, mules, llamas, et cetera, carrying provisions along the trails . . . and unfortunately leaving a trail of their own behind

point-to-point	a vehicle shuttle (or similar assistance) is required for this type of route, which is ridden from the designated trailhead to a distant location, or endpoint, where the route ends; total mileage is for the one-way trip from trailhead to endpoint
portage	to carry your bike on your person
pummy	volcanic activity in the Pacific Northwest and elsewhere produces soil with a high content of pumice: trails through such soil often become thick with dust, but this is light in consistency and can usually be pedaled; remember, however, to pedal carefully, for this dust obscures whatever might lurk below
quads	bikers use this term to refer both to the extensor muscle in the front of the thigh (which is separated into four parts) and to USGS maps; the expression "Nice quads!" refers always to the former, however, except in those instances when the speaker is an engineer
runoff	rainwater or snowmelt
scree	an accumulation of loose stones or rocky debris lying on a slope or at the base of a hill or cliff
signed	a "signed" trail has signs in place of blazes
single-track	a single, narrow path through grass or brush or over rocky terrain, often created by deer, elk, or backpackers; single-track riding is some of the best fun around
slickrock	the rock-hard, compacted sandstone that is *great* to ride and even prettier to look at; you'll appreciate it even more if you think of it as a petrified sand dune or seabed (which it is), and if the rider before you hasn't left tire marks (from unnecessary skidding) or granola bar wrappers behind
snowmelt	runoff produced by the melting of snow
snowpack	unmelted snow accumulated over weeks or months of winter—or over years in high-mountain terrain
spur	a road or trail that intersects the main trail you're following
squid	one who skids
switchback	a zigzagging road or trail designed to assist in traversing steep terrain: mountain bikers should *not* skid through switchbacks

talus	the rocky debris at the base of a cliff, or a slope formed by an accumulation of this rocky debris
technical	terrain that is difficult to ride due not to its grade (steepness) but to its obstacles—rocks, logs, ledges, loose soil . . .
topo	short for topographical map, the kind that shows both linear distance *and* elevation gain and loss; "topo" is pronounced with both vowels long
trashed	a trail that has been destroyed (same term used no matter what has destroyed it . . . cattle, horses, or even mountain bikers riding when the ground was too wet)
two-wheel-drive	this refers to any vehicle with drive-wheel capability on only two wheels (a passenger car, for instance, has two-wheel-drive); a two-wheel-drive road is a road or trail easily traveled by an ordinary car
water bar	an earth, rock, or wooden structure that funnels water off trails to reduce erosion
washboarded	a road that is surfaced with many ridges spaced closely together, like the ripples on a washboard; these make for very rough riding, and even worse driving in a car or jeep
whoop-de-doo	closely spaced dips or undulations in a trail; these are often encountered in areas traveled heavily by ORVs
wilderness area	land that is officially set aside by the federal government to remain *natural*—pure, pristine, and untrammeled by any vehicle, including mountain bikes; though mountain bikes had not been born in 1964 (when the United States Congress passed the Wilderness Act, establishing the National Wilderness Preservation system), they are considered a "form of mechanical transport" and are thereby excluded; in short, stay out
wind chill	a reference to the wind's cooling effect upon exposed flesh; for example, if the temperature is 10 degrees Fahrenheit and the wind is blowing at 20 miles per hour, the wind chill (that is, the actual temperature to which your skin reacts) is *minus* 32 degrees; if you are riding in wet conditions things are even worse, for the wind-chill would then be *minus 74 degrees!*
windfall	anything (trees, limbs, brush, fellow bikers) blown down by the wind

An active member of the Joliet Bicycle Club, Dave Shepherd travels both off-road and on-road when not writing his "Musings From the Back of the Peloton" humor column for the club newsletter. Dave is an associate with Hale Associates, a management consulting firm in Western Springs, Illinois. He lives in Plainfield, Illinois with his wife, Terri, his two sons, Ian and Kyle, and of course, his Alaskan Malamute, Timber Mist the Devil's Voice, more affectionately known as Astro.

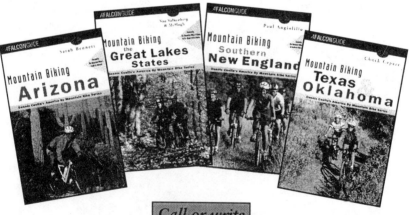
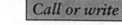

FALCON GUIDES

HIKE it

HIKER'S GUIDES

Hiker's Guide to Alaska
Hiking Alberta
Hiking Arizona
Hiking Arizona's Cactus Country
Hiking the Beartooths
Hiking Big Bend National Park
Hiking California
Hiking Carlsbad Caverns
    and Guadalupe National Parks
Hiking Colorado
Hiker's Guide to Florida
Hiking Georgia
Hiking Glacier/Waterton Lakes National Park
Hiking Hot Springs
    in the Pacific Northwest
Hiking Idaho
Hiking Maine
Hiking Michigan
Hiking Montana
Hiker's Guide to Montana's
    Continental Divide Trail
Hiking Nevada
Hiking New Hampshire
Hiking New Mexico
Hiking North Carolina
Hiker's Guide to Oregon
Hiking Oregon's Eagle Cap Wilderness
Hiking Olympic National Park
Hiking Tennessee
Hiking Texas
Hiking Utah

Hiking Virginia
Hiking Washington
Hiker's Guide to Wyoming
Hiking Northern Arizona
Trail Guide to Bob Marshall Country
Wild Montana

ROCK CLIMBER'S GUIDES

Rock Climbing Colorado
Rock Climbing Montana
Rock Climbing Texas & Oklahoma

DENNIS COELLO'S
AMERICA BY MOUNTAIN BIKE SERIES

Mountain Biking Arizona
Mountain Biker's Guide to Central Appalachia
Mountain Biker's Guide to Colorado
Mountain Biking the Great Lake States
Mountain Biking the Great Plains States
Mountain Biking the Midwest
Mountain Biking New Mexico
Mountain Biker's Guide to
    Northern California/Nevada
Mountain Biking Northern New England
Mountain Biker's Guide to Ozarks
Mountain Biking the Pacific Northwest
Mountain Biking the Southeast
Mountain Biker's Guide to Southern California
Mountain Biking Southern New England
Mountain Biking Texas and Oklahoma
Mountain Biker's Guide to Utah
Mountain Biking the Midwest

■ *To order any of these books, or to request an expanded list of available titles, including guides for viewing wildlife, birding, scenic driving, or rockhounding, please call 1-800-582-2665, or write to Falcon, PO Box 1718, Helena, MT 59624.*